THE
OLD HOUSE A

The

OLD HOUSE AT COATE

and other essays

BY RICHARD JEFFERIES

Edited with Biographical Notes
by
SAMUEL J. LOOKER

Wood Engravings by
AGNES MILLER PARKER

Ex Libris Press

First published 1948 by Lutterworth Press

This edition published 1985 by

Ex Libris Press
1 The Shambles
Bradford on Avon
Wiltshire

Cover by 46 Design, Bradford on Avon

Printed by A.Wheaton and Co., Exeter

ISBN 0 9506563 8 0

Publisher's Note The text of *The Old House at Coate* follows the Lutterworth edition exactly although the Introduction, Notes and bibliography which appeared in the earlier edition have been omitted here - it was thought that these were of more interest to the scholar than to the general reader. A shortened version of the Biographical Notes (without the footnotes) has been retained, and footnotes in the present text are those of the original editor Samuel J. Looker. The present publisher would like to express appreciation of Mr Looker's painstaking task as editor of this collection and to thank Lutterworth Press for permission to reprint in this form.

Agnes Miller Parker (1895-1980) was born in Ayrshire, Scotland, studied at Glasgow School of Art and taught herself to engrave on wood in the 1920s. Commissions followed and her reputation grew, particularly in the subjects of landscapes and rural life. In addition to Jefferies and others, she illustrated works by H.E.Bates, Thomas Hardy and an edition of A.E. Housman's *A Shropshire Lad*.

Contents

Notes on the Contents

(From Samuel Looker's Introduction and Notes in the 1948 edition)

The Old House at Coate Jefferies had written *The Story of my Heart* which was rather an autobiography of the mind when he planned a more factual kind of description of his early life, an account more especially of the surroundings of his old home in Wiltshire. *The Old House at Coate* represents this unfinished project.

The Country Near London The first and second pieces were written when Jefferies lived in Surbiton, around 1880, before it was engulfed in the spreading London suburbs.

The Strength of the English and *The Squire and the Land* represent unfinished portions of a book that Jefferies planned and intended to write entitled *The History of the English Squire*.

Biographical Notes

I

RICHARD JEFFERIES was a West Countryman who spent the first twenty-nine years of his life in the same neighbourhood. He was born at Coate Farmhouse, in Coate, in 1848. Coate was a small hamlet, a mile or two from the town of Swindon, on the Hungerford Road. The son of a farmer, and the descendant of a long line of farming folk—although he himself never cared for practical farming—Jefferies inherited a love of the countryside and a paternal passion for the acquirement of rustic lore. His father, James Luckett Jefferies, the Mr. Iden of *Amaryllis at the Fair*, was a man of very marked individuality. The unforgettable and masterly portrait of him, in the early chapters of *Amaryllis*, shows how deeply his strange, and in some ways enigmatic, personality had impressed itself upon the plastic mind of his son. James Luckett's influence, not always to the good, was, indeed, very great; but Richard did owe to his father much active encouragement and information on country life and cognate matters.

The life at Coate Farmhouse was not an easy one, especially for a temperament like that of Richard Jefferies. There must have been a certain conflict of wills and interests. Mr. and Mrs. Jefferies were not happily mated. Money was very short and became increasingly so as time went on. James Luckett, himself almost a genius, a queer original, yet in many ways an unpractical dreamer, was married to Elizabeth, not a lover of the country or of farm life, and who had lost what love she ever possessed for James, of whose thoughts and habits she had grown severely critical and even censorious. Here were all the elements of married unhappiness.

Richard Jefferies, a delicate youth, who was then, and remained throughout his whole life, a shy, proud and independent solitary, avid for knowledge, but not always wise in his own personal concerns and beliefs, yet intensely, almost morbidly, sensitive, was not likely to be entirely at ease or happy in so strange a milieu. Certainly, he was unlikely to find much real sympathy or understanding from either of his parents. No man deeply attached to his mother, or who even thought highly of her, could have painted the picture of Mrs. Iden in *Amaryllis*.

This strange, difficult household had, however, one great advantage for Jefferies. In his boyhood and early youth, the formative years, he was left for long periods very much to his own devices. He wandered over the fields, hills and woods of his native countryside, and these rambles were a more vital schooling and acquirement of knowledge for what he was to do and become in the world than any amount of academic learning. His official schooling was, indeed, but intermittent. However, Richard, as his note-books, and the general range of knowledge displayed in his published writings show, became a highly educated person, with a quite unusual range of information. Apart from his country wandering and meditation, he was an indefatigable reader of good books, with a very great intellectual curiosity and passionate desire for knowledge. It was now, too, that he first began to indulge in those almost esoteric feelings and thoughts which afterwards found a voice in *The Story of My Heart*.

At seventeen years of age, Jefferies became a reporter on a Swindon newspaper, and was soon employed on all the multifarious duties of a junior member of the staff in a small country town. Later on, he joined the staff of *The Wilts and Gloucestershire Standard*, which was published at Cirencester, and remained with the paper for several years. Soon he began to try to write fiction, with indifferent success. Some short stories from his pen had already appeared in the Swindon newspaper, and in 1873 and 1875 respectively, at his own expense, *The Scarlet Shawl* and *Restless Human Hearts* were published by Tinsley. Both books were practically worthless. *World's End*, which appeared in Tinsley's list for 1877, the year in which Jefferies moved to Surbiton, was slightly better. But these three books did not suggest that Richard Jefferies was born to be a novelist. His plots were unreal and melodramatic, his dialogue often jejune, his characters mere pasteboard. The books were, in fact, a failure. Later on, in *Greene Ferne Farm* (1880), *The Dewy Morn* (1884), and *Amaryllis at the Fair* (1887), he came to realize and display his strength as a novelist. This is shown in those eloquent and fascinating chapters on bucolic life, and in the wonderful character studies of Farmer Iden, Alere Flamma, Felise and Amaryllis. These at least enable the reader to form an attractive idea of Jefferies as a novelist.

It was in 1872, when twenty-four years of age, that Jefferies first achieved some measure of success. The occasion of this was the publication by *The Times* of two letters on the condition of the Wiltshire labourer.

Biographical Notes

These had been first offered to and refused by *The Standard*, a newspaper we may see by a remark in *Amaryllis* that Jefferies' own family were in the habit of taking, and to which, later on, he was himself to contribute many excellent nature essays and sketches. *The Times* not only published the letters but wrote a leader on the subject which led to discussion, and brought Jefferies' name to the favourable notice of other editors.

This publicity soon opened up avenues of work elsewhere. He found that editors of the monthlies were glad to take his essays of country life. *Fraser's Magazine*, *Chambers's Journal*, *The Standard*, *The Pall Mall Gazette*, and *Longman's Magazine*, all began to print his work, and before long he was able to begin the publication of his collected volumes of country lore, on which his fame chiefly rests.

The remainder of Jefferies' short and outwardly uneventful history is soon told. He married a neighbouring farmer's daughter, Miss Jessie Baden of Daye House Farm, and by her had three children, two boys and a girl, but one of the boys died in infancy. After he left Wiltshire, he lived at Surbiton, Eltham, Brighton, Crowborough, and finally, at Goring-on-Sea, near Worthing, where he died in 1887. His health, never very robust, broke down in 1882, and although afterwards he had comparatively short interludes free from pain, he was never really well. His last essays, and his best, were dictated to his wife when he was too weak to hold a pen.

Richard Jefferies is buried at Broadwater Cemetery, on the outskirts of Worthing, where the grave of an equally great naturalist, that of W. H. Hudson, may also be found.

THE OLD HOUSE AT COATE

Chapter 1

THE BLUE DOORS

THE old house at Coate, a little hamlet in Wiltshire, was shut off from the road by a solid stone wall, the general entrance being through double doors. They were called the blue doors, as that was the colour of the paint, and were between six and seven feet high. A favourite greyhound, when these doors (being hung on an incline) had closed behind his master, used to clear them at a bound, his paws seeming but just to touch the top so lightly did he go over. As the cross-bars slowly decayed and became hollow in places, robins and wrens came to them several times in the day for the insects. The tiny brown wrens appear to have their regular rounds, visiting the same spot day after day and always singing on the same perches. One used to sing on the top of these doors, and then passing on, first to the eaves of the cowshed, next to a heap of stones, where he slipped through the interstices, then to some logs piled against the wall, sang again when he reached the woodpile, perched on the topmost faggot.

The eave-swallows dropping from their nests under the thatch and gaining impetus from the downward slide seemed as if they must strike the broad doors, but suddenly rising with sleight-of-wing passed over upwards into the buoyant air.

Intangible at hand, the blue yonder above the fields and the trees, like an ethereal lake, sustains these feathered swimmers with such ease that a stroke sends them an arrow's flight.

13

The Old House at Coate

The doors were so high that when near them nothing could be seen beyond but the clouds, so that the sky seemed to linger at once, and the swallows rising over to dart with it. They faced the north, and the north side kept its paint well, but the inner southern side, burnt by the summer sun, and receiving the driving southern rain, decayed twice as fast.

The wagtails usually came, too, over these doors, uttering their call as they jerked up and down: the whole circuit of the place was open to them, yet they generally entered here. They were among the most constant of the residents, the dependents of the house. As they say in classical times, the slaves and the slaves' children, generation after generation, were sheltered by the same portico; so, though free to go wherever their wings can carry them, many species of birds cling to the homestead. Their nests are near it, they roost close at hand; by day they go out into the fields and forage but return every two or three hours, and are sure to meet some of their mates at the old place.

Opposite the blue doors, across the road, was a stile, and a footpath leading to a cattleyard, called the Lower Pen. That field was used for grazing, and rarely mown, so that there were generally cows in it. The wagtails, fond of feeding about cattle, jerking their tails up and down close to their very noses, got into the habit of leaving the homestead over the doors in this direction. First visiting the cows, and perhaps riding a few minutes on one's back, they went next to the yard at the Lower Pen, and presently returned the way they had come. They thus established a route, and continued to follow it.

The Blue Doors

The legs of the wagtail are so slender that they scarce seem capable of sustaining even its light weight; each appears a mere black line; the plumage is shaded with delicate precision, and every tiny feather besides that side or tip that meets the eye is equally carefully marked underneath, and where it cannot be observed, so much "work" is there, so much thorough honesty in nature's

art. Everything out of sight is as tenderly touched as that open to the passing view.

The wagtails, like the ibis, were sacred; they were never shot or disturbed; wagtails, swallows, swifts, turtle-doves, yellow-hammers, robins, wrens, green plovers, and even thrushes, if not semi-sacred were rarely fired at.

One of the large blue doors was often "hapsed", i.e. hasped open to the wall, for convenience of entrance and exit; but, when it was closed, the private road within made a pleasant ambulatory. On one side, the high wall of the front garden and of the house itself: on the other, that of the cattle-sheds, formed a kind of hollow way, shut at the end by the doors; these walls and doors kept off the hard easterly winds of spring, while the sunshine at midday filled the place with light and warmth. Walking up and down here, taking care not to go too near the doors, for some little draught, of course, drew over them as a wind draws back over a wood, the position of the sun could be marked as he rose higher day by day towards that degree which fills the fields with flowers. In winter, his disk but just cleared the top of the great oak, the largest in the first hedgerow southwards. Now he was as far again above the horizon, and the swallows were here—with no thought of nest-building, yet they come every now and then to perch on the ledge of the chimney (but just able to face the keen east) and twitter to each other. Another place they used to perch on was the ridge of the cattle-shed running parallel to the house. It was thatched, and, in course of time decaying, the sticks which are driven through the straw stood out an inch or so in a row along the summit of the roof. These little projections suited them; half a dozen or more sometimes settled there, marshalled in single file.

There were some very long willow poles leaning against the faggot pile; the points standing up high and isolated were continually visited by the swallows; so was the top of a tall pear in the orchard and an egg-plum tree; also the narrow steep ridge of the slated stable. All round the house they had their resting places, where they met to converse, or stayed to sing. They did not alight on trees in the hedgerows or copses; only close at home.

Walking to and fro here (the roadway was dry and firm underfoot), when going towards the doors and facing the north, the sky looked hard; and the elms by the Lower Pen could be seen to swing before the wind. On turning, the sunshine—the light itself seems warm—

met me with its delicious touch: it is like bathing in a more delicate element; the southern sky was refulgent and could scarcely be gazed at; the grass of the meadow (on which the roadway opened after passing the buildings) was green, and the hedge on its right side budding into leaf.

The growth of the year from spring into summer is beautiful to watch. But when the north winds came and the lower sky and the trees appeared dark—everything darkens when the north wind blows, and the nights are black—this covered way was no longer tenable. It rushed straight through, making no account of the high doors; it came over and under and through them, and cleared every dead leaf and fibre and particle of dust, sweeping the place clean. The refrain of the wind sound changing—each page—with the seasons.

Then, turning to the left, I found some shelter behind the cart-house, and stable wall: not so good a strolling place, but better than none. If the breeze shifted south or west, quarters often cold in winter and spring, when the air blows full of moisture, there still remained the "paving", as it was called: a broad footpath flagged by the house on the north side.

The swallows flew underneath, low down over the surface of the road. High as the great blue doors were, this leafy loophole flanked them. Years ago, it seemed an event when the second door was opened, not without labour, for the passage of the waggon. It had to be heaved off the central block,   swung back, and propped there with the   iron bar attached to it. The waggon came rolling in with a load of hay; wisps caught against the ivy; against the eaves even; the heavy weight made a deep sound, between the walls; the load, as it passed,

17

shut out the light momentarily from the windows that fronted to the hollow way, and the top rose nearly level on to the roof there above the swallows' nests under the thatch.

Chapter 2

THE SEASONS AND THE STARS

THE sun rose in summer almost by the elms at the Lower Pen—across the road—so much to the north of east, and sank in the evening down the road which ran east and west, so that then the blue doors were shone on early in the morning for half an hour on their northern side; and one part (the rest being shaded by the projecting wall) I think was just touched by the sunset rays.

Seeing the sun thus day by day traverse the sky about the house, passing the fixed points corresponding to the compass, and changing her position with the seasons— so that the house, the garden, and the trees about it made one large sidereal dial—made the solar apparent motion and the phenomena of the heavens very real and almost tangible.

In summer, no matter how early in the morning we went to the corner of the wall, under the lime and the fir, to look over, there was the sun already high above the elms. He had started from over the level plain: rising with boldest curve almost to the zenith, the shadow of the house then scarcely covered the "paving", and the moss on the northern slope of the thatched roof was dry under his beams: white and pulsing with heat, he looked   straight down upon us: then descending steeply, as if it were a hill, he paused over the elms on Smith Field, and finally sank to the north of them, leaving but a mere notch of the earth to go under before the morning.

The Old House at Coate

It looked about ten miles only from the spot where the disk went down to where it rose; and all the night, from half past ten till one o'clock, there was a faint white light just above where he travelled beneath. At a little after one it was lost in the fast coming dawn. The circle of the sun was almost visible; there was but a short arc wanting to complete it; and thus we saw and understood that the sun never sets.

And the advance of the sun up from the south, wheeling further towards us day by day as the spring came on: and the retreat, wheeling further away as the autumn came, was plain from the time when the disk just cleared—as I have said—the great oak in the first hedgerow to the south, till it rose and sank north of the line of the roadway, and at midday looked down right over the house. Here was the centre of the world, the sun swung round us; we rode at night straight away into the space of the stars.

On a dry summer night, when there was no dew, I used to lie down on my back at full length (looking to the east), on the grass footpath by the orchard, and gaze up into the sky. This is the only way to get at it and feel the stars: while you stand upright, the eye, and through the eye, the mind, is biased by the usual aspect of things: the house there, the trees yonder; it is difficult to forget the mere appearance of rising and setting. Looking straight up like this, from the path to the stars, it was clear and evident that I was really riding among them; they were not above, nor all round, but I was in the midst of them. There was no underneath, no above: everything was on a level with me; the sense of measurement and distance disappeared.

As one walks in a wood, with trees all about, so then

by day (when the light only hid them) I walked amongst the stars. I had not got then to leave this world to enter space: I was already there. The vision is indeed contracted, nor can we lift our feet further than the earth; yet we are really among these things to-day. The eye sees further at night than at noon. But though the

bright light of noon intervenes like a mist or cloud, still the stars are there, space is there and we are in the midst of it. The touch of the sun's rays seemed to make me feel to the sun: the sight of the stars, to make me feel to them.

Gazing up from the footpath at the points of light overhead, and at the openings between where the mind looks into space itself, there was nothing between me and them, nor between me and the sun. They were as much a part of my existence as the elms across the road, the house, the blue doors, the cattle-shed, the meadow, and the brook. They were no more separated than the furniture of the parlour; no more isolated than the table, the old, old chair where I used to sit, as it stood by the southern window, watching for the first star over the mulberry tree. The old chair was the furniture of the room; the elms and the grass and the bank were the furniture of the earth; the stars and the sun and the deep sky, the limitless ether, were only the continuation. There is no break, no chasm, between here and there; nothing to step over in the darkness of an inscrutable to-morrow. The light comes to us—the physical light —in that   alone there is a connexion; the ether, too, extends; as for the mind, it can and does go farther than this. It does not require an ascent; we are there already. I have never felt so much myself, an individual, as a part of this whole. In the summer night, lying thus upon the grass, the faint, yet distinct, pole star shone on my left above an ash tree growing in the hedgerow across the road. It was always there, and still: but the stars of the Great Bear moved, and some of them (all the stars of the Lesser Bear) never sank: they revolved about the pole and never went under the horizon. From the Lesser Bear, which is the nearest, to the Great Bear is one step—a wider ring; from thence to Capella or Arcturus, a yet wider; and so on to the zenith and the south.

Thus I realized that none of the stars (nor the sun) ever rose or sank: and that gave the feeling of being among them. The sward on which I was lying, the orchard behind, the house, the white wall of the garden (the horse steadily feeding in the meadow), the elms, the blue doors and roadway, the cattle-shed, and the stile, with myself, were in the same stream of space.

In winter, at the beginning of the year, Orion rose up the road and over it, his huge glittering frame athwart the highway: then the Pleiades, a startled flock of sheep timidly running together, were over the elms by the rickyard: Antares, in summer, was low to the south, by the same great oak the sun just cleared in December: Arcturus often hung, night after night, over the orchard: Donati's Comet came, first, a tiny speck with a faint spray of light behind it, over the elms opposite the orchard (they were a favourite perch of the starlings that built in the thatch of the house), its flaming brand afterwards started forth from the sunset every evening.

One night there was a comet (after Donati's, it only appeared a short time) whose immense but thin and misty tail spanned the sky like a thicker Milky Way with stars shining through it.

The new moon usually appeared first over the hollow oak by the brook in Smith Field. The trees and the constellations were grouped together: by the boughs the march of Orion westward, as the spring went on, till he overtook the sun, was visible every night. Every year, at the same time, the same star shone through the same tree. The position of many of them, by day, was as well known to me as if I could have seen them: it was only to describe an imaginary arc from the top of the ash. The highest elm is but a little plant on the surface of the earth: no more than groundsel—a mere weed; you can see over the groundsel and the highest tree equally well. And the stars were but just above the ash and the oak— never far off, and always there.

The line of the sunlight, the edge between the

shadow and the white beam, on the side of the window-frame in the parlour—the southern window—moved every day. If I drew a pencil-mark along that line to-day, at two o'clock, and to-morrow, at two o'clock, there was a slight change; in a week, the mark was left far behind. Thus far, then, thus far subtended by the distance to the sun, my blue doors, and roadway, and mulberry tree and orchard, and meadow, had moved among the stars. I was among them already.

In the morning, the shadows of the elms by the rick-yard on the east side of the roadway extended almost across the meadow: at noon, in summer, even the wide-spreading oak in the first hedgerow to the south scarcely darkened the grass beneath it; from a distance, the shadow was imperceptible—it did not, apparently, extend beyond the verge of the boughs. In the evening, the ashes and elms and oaks in the western hedge returned their shadows back across again to the rickyard.

As the seasons changed, the shadows moved round the field, only avoiding the northern end by the house. The shadows, too, as of the carthouse across the roadway, of the walnut tree   where the roadway opened on   the meadow, the slant from   the garden wall across the blue doors: these shadows, too, every day and all day long, declared the motion, and the motion the inseparable connexion between the heavens and the ground under-foot. It was impossible to get away from it for a moment. If, while thinking of other things, I chanced to see a sunbeam on the wall: if I see it now, it instantly recalls the same feeling. Put your hand on it—you touch the sun; and know that you are as much in the ether, in space, as the sun itself.

Sometimes, at the northern end of my walk to and

fro the roadway, looking over the blue doors, I saw the pale north sky from which the north wind rushed down and shook them, rattling the latch. Sometimes, returning to the other end, I saw the woods on the low hill southwards, two miles away, become hidden by a mist like cloud; in three minutes the shower came driving up.

Or, another time, pausing by the wall of the house—for anything high helps you to look up—there were flecks of curling cloud, at an immense elevation, scarce moving, and hardly obscuring the blue—no more than lace.

Occasionally the white moon appeared in the azure sky of noonday. Again there was a faint mist, northwards over the blue doors; southwards, over the wooded slope; westwards (seen through the apple trees), over the slope there; eastwards, too—just a glimpse between the butts of the elms of the downs in that direction. A soft, delicious, mist—the summer air made visible—a mist that ripens the corn and fixes the fruit. Lie down, then, in the shadow, on the grass, in drowsy luxury.

There were loopholes in the trees, and openings between the buildings, look-out places from which in a moment I knew the state of the atmosphere—they answered to the compass, they were fixed points of the observatory. But the view through each of these windows of the trees went farther than the fields, or the woods on the hills. The wind that came from the west through the apple trees, with scudding clouds and stormy sunsets lighting up the place with rosy glow, I could seem to see its course from rocky Cornwall, from the mountainous billows of the Atlantic, and yet farther and farther than the clear broad rivers of the new world, the vast Pacific opened its expanse.

Towards the east, lifting on tiptoe to glance over the blue doors, the blast which drove up in the face as if it were splashed with water, I could see its course, over the darkened fields and brooks, from the grey north sea, from the narrow inlets and fir woods of Scandinavia, and still east and north to the unknown ice. Southwards, through the rain mist that shut out the woods upon the hills, I could see the Solent, the green channel, the wide fields of France, the blue inland sea, the sands of Africa.

Like a vast plain seen from a hill the surface of the earth stretched around: it was mapped out from this, the centre, so vivid was the sense of seeing the whole. Yet, with all its size, it was small: too small.

I have always hoped that some day our voyagers will find the earth larger than is thought. I hope there are new continents somewhere: interminable forests, and mountains that will take a century to climb. With all its width, it seems so small: and it becomes less, daily, as we traverse it so easily. But it must always have been small to the thought. Scandinavia was just beyond the stile and the Lower Pen; Africa, just beyond the wooded slope; America, yonder over the bank. So large, and yet so little; so many thousand miles, yet seen at a glance in an instant.

Lying upon the sward at midnight, and looking up, as I have said, I felt but a speck: the house, the fields, the surface of the earth, stretching around, was scarce more than a clod rushing through space. There never seemed to me any distinction between day and night: it is a mere succession of light and shadow; but existence is continuous and knows no break. Neither is there any difference between the days: or, indeed, the years, or the centuries; it is all alike (I mean, to me); and what is meant by dates I could never grasp.

But though the great earth is small, the merest atom of lichen on the garden wall bounding the roadway, grey, rough to the touch, and fixed to the stone, is as real, it exists, and *is*, as much as if it filled half the visible horizon. It is very curious to touch anything; it is as if the soul thereby ascertained the existence of matter. From these windows of the trees, then, the world could be seen as well as the fields.

Chapter 3

BIRDS AND PEOPLE

IN December, walking to and fro the roadway, from the blue doors to the walnut tree at the entrance to the meadow, as the afternoon drew on to four o'clock the sparrows began to come to the thick ivy round about the fir tree in the corner of the wall. They came, too, to the ivy about the gable of the low roof over the window (which the waggon darkened with its load as it passed). The mass of leaves sheltered them like a cloak. The wrens went to the hayricks under the eaves of the thatch, to the holes the sparrows had made in the eaves of the sheds. Sometimes, in hard frost, the blackbirds came there, too—they could not find warmth in the hedges—and the sky, as the dusk deepened, was left to the wild-fowl.

In June, and while the summer was at its height, there were always birds awake: the cuckoo did not cease till the stars came; nor did the swallows finally settle—they were both about again before the dawn; the thrushes sang right into the darkness, and again before the travelling shadow of night departed. I love the night, and I was always late—the last to pass the blue doors; but, return whenever I would, there was then always some bird awake.

The blue doors were banging ceaselessly, from dawn to midnight: that is, the one that was latched was for ever being opened and closing of its own weight. First to enter in the dawn (there is scarce time in summer for the dawn, so softly does the morning come) were

28

the mowers. Then the milkers, then folk for water from the pump—thrown open to all who liked to use it; then the haymakers, their children, waggons, carts, callers; just before noon, women going home for half an hour to adjacent cottages and coming back again to work: and so on till evening, and more than ever then for water again. From half past two in the morning till nine or ten at night the blue doors banged incessantly: after that they slammed occasionally up to midnight. They opened to the highway which ran east and west into the world.

Westwards, down the hill, it was overhung by the group of elms opposite the orchard; eastwards, where level and straight, it was bordered by a line of oaks. There were meadows on either side, and wide hedge-rows. The rooks flew idly, ever cawing; the swallows, up and down; the chaffinches called on the boughs; sometimes a weasel ran across it; in the night, some-times a fox slipped along. But it was the highway: westwards down the hill it went, by the bridge over the brook, into the world; eastwards, the boughs of the trees concealed its course, but still it went out among men.

Waggons with corn and hay and straw, or returning with coal; carts; traps; conveyances of every kind; steam-ploughing engines; gipsies' vans; horsemen; men on foot; someone and something was always drifting by.

Come to the look-out corner under the lilac, the fir and the lime boughs, when you would, the road was never quite vacant; either up it or down it there was someone advancing. From the east, the carthorses sud-denly appeared from under the shadow of the trees: from the west, they came round the curve by the bridge and toiled up the hill, the skin on their plump flanks creasing as they strained. Well-known figures, recognized even before their shape was defined, came along the level: if the road seemed for a moment empty, the next someone stood out from the lane close by, or the gate of the waggon track further up; or children crept out from under the bushes of the hedge.

From the villages along the verge of the Downs, from the hill-towns, to and fro people were always passing: stolid waggoners, counting their steps till the same old inn was reached where they always stopped; whether the ale was good or indifferent mattered not at all, having stayed once they stayed again; for human nature finds a pleasure in doing again what it has done before, though the reason has long since departed.

Within, when the great blue doors were shut, it was private and enclosed, quite apart, and all was shut off with high walls; when they were open, they opened on the world. The road went eastwards, 78 miles to London; westwards, 40 miles to Bristol; it bent at the cross roads (there is no human place of habitation without cross roads), 60 miles through Salisbury to the Solent; a lane (once a Roman highway) went straight from thence to the north. Lost as the hamlet was, it was not separated or divided: there was the world of the villages and hill-towns round about, a province of themselves; there was the greater world beyond, from which two things came and went—the beggars and the mails: the beggars afoot, the letters passed in the cart.

If in the summer afternoon the road was alone, white with heated rays, without shadow, and dusty: if it was vacant and deserted, and all the folk scattered in the meadows among the rustling hay, still there was a foot

coming, the heel and the ball of the toe pressing the dust
—naked outside the shoe and stocking—a foot coming,
not by wheels or machinery, but by sinews: a naked
foot, measuring and diminishing the distance. By and
by, the misery of the world would pass. If the broad
moon shone among the elms, and the shadowy road was
silent and still, even then there was someone coming:
the lover returning from the trysting-place; the poacher
slipping across from one field to another; the drunkard
drifting homewards, muttering to himself.

Less than a hamlet, it was not separated: in the still-
ness, you could hear the roll of the trains in the deep
cutting two or three miles distant; and sometimes, in
the day (in bare winter) the white curl of steam; the
whistle came echoing, long-drawn and hollow, in the
midst of the summer day. Less than a hamlet, these high
walls and large blue doors, and jealous shade, of limes
and fir and delicious single lilac, were not—could not
—be alone.

Weary men retire early to sleep: at eleven on a
summer night, after the labour of the day, the place was
still: the road, to all appearance, empty; the broad moon
shone on oak and ash. Presently, there came an indistinct tapping: was it the door, swung by a light gust of
wind? Did something fall? It came again, sharp and
defined: it was hoofs; quicker and quicker, round the
corner, down the hill, out from the shadow, along the
level where the moonlight fell: the rapid mailcart,
rattling, tandem style, to catch the train, and commu-
nicate with the greater world, seventy-eight miles away.
He used to draw up his horses on their haunches for my
letters: it was well and cleverly done; only a little while
to midnight, and the next morning before breakfast

they were faithfully delivered without miss of sorting or loss.

Less than a hamlet, lost in the trees and meadows, yet not apart or alone. So the great blue doors banged, from the mowers at half past two in the dawn to the mail at half past eleven: and later still, for I loved the night and idled it away as much as possible. There were the stars. Along the road on the hill, at the open and exposed spot where it was raised to mend a hollow, by the White Rails, you could see the whole sky, from the farthest east to the farthest west, the north and south. There was no better view, even on a peak.

In spring, there was the fragrance of the may: in the hedge opposite the orchard, by the care of the master, the hawthorn bush which flowered so finely was always left when the fence was trimmed. The golden chain drooped its bloom over the orchard wall: the lilac timidly appeared at the corner: there was a horse-chestnut by the stile; one or other was in bloom, or the orchard itself—all pink and white. The nightingale sang at the top of the first meadow: down by the withy bed the brook sparrow chattered; when I came round the house, sometimes the swallows just spoke to one another.

You might find a strawberry, by moonlight, kneeling on the sward, and lifting the leaves; or press the sweet-briar as you passed. Then the grassy footpath by the orchard: and, lying at full length, gazing up, the stars went over; and, when at last indoors, it was not long before the window-pane was all aglow with the morning.

Chapter 4

UNDER THE APPLE TREE

UNDER the russet apple tree there was a seat made of a broad plank set on a low upright at each end. It was placed on the north side of the tree so that there was some shadow till the sun sank towards Ladderhill. The heat of the afternoon beams in summer fell full upon it, and had split it at one end, but beneath and at the side to the north the lichen grew. The grass rose up, tall and green, about the uprights, in the shadow of the plank: the seat seemed to rest on the top of the blades. Immediately westwards, within two feet, the wall of a ha-ha sank to the Brook Field, the meadow by the brook: from the hollow to the ha-ha the meadow soon began to slope down to the stream, about a hundred yards away. Meadow after meadow succeeded; another brook came down to join the first, then trees; and three or more miles away the steep down at Ladderhill marked the horizon. There was nothing inside between the russet apple and the down, but the meadows, the hollow oak, the hedges, and the afternoon sun.

The wooden seat, scorched by the full beams, was untenable then, in summer: it was a morning and evening resort. While the dew glistened on the mowing grass under the ha-ha, then in the shadow of the apple bloom, I used to sit there and look at the buttercups which grew thick and strong where the ground rose from the foot of the wall. They are flowers of the sun; they do not shrink from the fierce heat; they bloom finest where the sunshine is uninterrupted by shadow from morn till even.

The violets delight in quiet places, often under boughs or near the hedges: the buttercups stand up under the sky. The dew does not stay long upon them: the drops so high up soon disappear in the air; the trembling air flows in wavelets round about them; heat makes its motion visible at a distance.

On the grass low down on the cool earth the dew remains till the rays fall straight upon it, but on these plants and their petals lifted up into the warm atmosphere it is gone before the first butterfly passes. Their hollow stems are stout enough to withstand the slight breeze by the ground and do not bend to it, but the upper and slenderer branches which bear the petals sway to each breath.

A greenfinch or a starling, rising hastily out of the grass, brushes a buttercup with his wings and shakes it while the rest are still. The roots are in the firm earth, fibres thrust between the crevices of the firm earth, the stem rises through the dewy grass; the cups are open, like a hollow palm, to the sun. A burnished surface on the petal reflects the rays: the pollen is a dull yellow, like gold dust in a quill. All day the sun burns down upon them, renewing their colour: by night, in the moon-beams, the field is still yellow; the rain does not change it; if a storm comes in darkness, the brighter the lightning, the clearer the colour of the flowers. At hand, they are separate and apart: yonder, they close together, and by the brook it is a general gold.

As the sun comes through the screen of the apple bloom, the heat is drawn off and his trail upon me is tender and dreamy: the strength and inflexibility of the frame which repulses repose slowly yields, and the mind, as the body slumbers, goes out and enters the larger life around.

This plant with golden petals has thrust its fibres into the crevices of the ground, which looks and feels firm,

but the solid clod is penetrable by the pushing finger of the root. The point is slender: the matter of which it is composed is incomparably more so; yet, fine as they are, there is still a division between the fibre and the earth. The earth is earth; the plant, plant—even at its tiniest tip, and at the smallest invisible fraction of its surface. The roots and their surface touch the particles of the earth, but they are still divided from them. Above the turf the leaves touch the air, but there is the same distinction. From the particles of the soil—if you cut the turf with a knife and take out a piece, you can crumble it and feel the particles between finger and thumb, though these, of course, are but coarse fragments, great rocks and boulders to the ultimate points of divisibility. Still, they are the smallest particles which the conscious sensitiveness of the skin can feel; and from these there passes into the fibre of the plant—into and through its surface—that essence, those particular and unseen atoms which are drawn up into and form its juice, or sap, from which its green tube is built, and from which presently emerges the golden bloom. From these points of contact (yet divided) with the earth and rain, the rain and the sunshine, the plant makes itself. The plant sucks in the atoms that fit its porous surface, that are attracted by and assimilated with it; thus the plant makes itself—the minaret builds itself. These atoms arrange that position towards each other by chemical attraction, or repulsion: by electric affinity; by yet more subtle forces which have no name.

I can see the minute particle arising from under the turf and, finally settling, transformed to a speck of golden dust in the sunshine above. Suppose the plant a mile high: suppose the atom the size of a boulder, one of the sarsens scattered about in these meadows, and weighing a ton: suppose it were actually visible, coursing up the vast tube and separating into the various components of green stem and golden flower: that the ultimate speck of golden dust were as large as an orange: that the subtle force which compelled the gigantic plant to thus build itself (the root acting on the earth, the earth on the root): that this subtle force were as plain and visible as water, and could be felt and its action known as certainly as that water runs downhill. One day, as the work of man goes on, the process of physical life will be thus plain and evident to the material eye. We shall certainly handle the life-force, the zoistic electricity, as we handle and know water: we shall see it crystallize the particles; we shall put it in motion ourselves and cause it to build the imitation of a plant. We shall not think it more wonderful than that very water whose existence has been the marvel of so many thoughtful ages. The water that runs there in the brook; the earth which I place my foot on; the air I breathe; the sunlight coming so softly through the apple bloom: these are the four miracles. They are astounding miracles: they are marvellous beyond expression.

Chapter 5

LIFE-FORCE, FLYING MACHINES

I TELL you, as I told you before, that to-day, this hour, we are among the stars. The imitation plant of future times will not be nearly so wonderful, for it will be only a combination—a putting together of things already existing; just as a machine is made of iron and brass, but the engineer did not construct the atoms of the original ore. The imitation plant will be a continuation: the subtle force already in existence: in the utilization of these there is no miracle, nor even a mystery. The life-force is, indeed, as common as water. There is no spot without it: the lichen starts up on the wall, and moss upon the ground; there is no spot as wide as one of those golden specks of dust without it. Its action is no more mystic than that of water running downhill. If in the many ages that have passed we have not arrived at the mode of handling it, it is for the most part because the idea, and the desire to do so, has not existed. First the idea: then the experiment; lastly, the realization.

The perfection of mere machines which now look simple enough has cost the world centuries of effort; but, having once got the idea, it was ultimately worked out.

Life-force will be thus worked out, and found, in the end, as common and as ordinary as water. For it is already so, being around (and in ourselves) everywhere; it is about us thicker than the dewdrops on the grass at dawn. There is no inaccessible secret in it any more than in water running down hill. It is in every one of these thousands upon thousands of buttercups: look, how common they are!

Have you ever walked in a fir wood and seen the incalculable millions of green needle-like leaves on the trees, and then stirred the ground and found it formed of these for a foot deep? How many of these in a thousand years?

Have you ever seen the little shells in marl—how many of these in five thousand years? These are visible to the naked eye: but then there is chalk and its history; how many creatures in ten thousand years?

Now, is not this life-force as common and ordinary as water? Like water, it will some day be used.

The sunbeams passing through a chink in the apple-bloom fall upon my hand, a streak across it: at first with light only; then with increasing heat. The buttercup—plant; the hand—flesh; but, in both plant and flesh, there is the same absorption of particles; the same attraction and repulsion arranging and separating them; the same or similar life-force doing its work, as water runs downhill. It is as common and as ordinary as that water; as the water in the brook yonder.

Of all the birds of the trees; the animals of the earth; the men of the houses; who shall tell the number? They are for number like the buttercups, the fir-needles, the shells, the makers of the chalk. In all these, the life-force —ordinary as water—has carried out its inevitable ends.

Whether it be one force, one thing; or whether, like the water, composed of more than one element, does not alter the fact in the least. Water does not feel, or think; neither does this force or forces; water is not soul, neither is this force or forces; it is not life itself—

life is a product, the result, let us say, of two or more points acting on each other, like the flame of fire; it is not life itself, it is only a force, possibly itself the result of some at present unknown physical bodies.

Life-force is not a secret, inviolable and sacred thing: it is as ordinary and common as water; and water is sacred, holy, and beautiful—a marvel and a miracle. So is a clod of earth. If a man, holding a clod of earth and looking into it and its potent and dormant powers, were to fall upon his knees he would not be an idolater. Neither would he before a dewdrop on the grass under the buttercups, or the fragrant scented rain that shakes off from the single lilac: or before this streak of light that falls across my hand: or this soft and delicious air that breathes up to me now and then from the brook. For all these are parts of the stars, amongst whom, as I say, we are already.

As, like water, this force, when better understood, will be used in building an imitation plant: so it will be used in building imitation flesh like this of my hand. Or if not so precisely then in the controlling and influencing of it.

I hope and pray it may be used for the good and benefit and beauty of the flesh: the physical bodies of human beings. That it will not be used merely as a motor to get from place to place—to carry us a thousand miles and deposit us, the same in ourselves as when we started. Such motors have their use and benefit. But the good I hope and pray from the ultimate discovery of the life-force or forces is that it may be employed to the actual, physical, flesh-good of the man and woman; to the strength and beauty of the limbs; to the increase of joy in living.

The Old House at Coate

Machinery is not the end of man: these times are bent almost too much on swift progress from place to place; and it is without doubt useful, but it is not all.

When the air is utilized, too, and ships sail among the clouds, then I hope at least attention will turn to man himself. A means of locomotion to the sun yonder, shining through the apple-bloom, would be wonderful, would yield wondrous results. But I am not looking to that. I have seen a child leap from this lichen wall, plunging into the buttercups, gathering them with shouts of joy, a glow on the face, and light in the eyes. That is what I want: more strength for the limbs; more and still more joy in living. To this end may the life-force or forces, when they are handled, be applied.

Chapter 6

THE BUTTERCUPS: FROM THE TREE TO
THE POOL

THE buttercups glow brighter as the sun ascends and the apple-bloom scarce shelters me. The dew in the grass beneath, from which the shadow of the wall has receded, is gone: and the swallows have passed still higher into the air—sometimes they seem to leave the meadows altogether; they must go higher than the elms and oaks; the air above the hills pleases them. Sometimes, again, they sweep low over the buttercups, so that their wings scarce escape a sprinkling of the golden dust.

If a petal chance to be touched by the thumb-nail in gathering the flower, the rude stylus leaves its mark—a streak, less bright, torn through the delicate surface. The fragments are on the thumb; minute as they are, where they lie, they hide the network of the skin.

All the valley of the brook is sunlight. I move always along the wooden seat still closer to the apple. Something in the atmosphere itself reflects the light; the air itself, like an infinitely diffused and intangible mist, hovers in the distant corners of the field.

A green fringe, the brook, marks the edge of the golden ground. The meadow on the other side is verdant with grass, and the heavy thick stems of marsh marigolds whose petals fell long since; but the brilliance of yellow ceases at the winding bank.

Beyond, another valley opens towards the apple tree; this, with the golden mead, runs north and south, or right and left;   that, east and west, so that its mouth faces this way. The hollow oak stands on the left slope, a luminous yet indistinct and indeterminable haze of sunlit atmosphere about it; the right slope rises higher and higher, with sheep grazing and horses, their heads uphill.

As I gaze I think of the great hill where so often in the old days I watched the red clouds of the morning, inhaling deeply. On this hill I used to bury my face in the thyme and listen to the song of the lark.

Through the hollow of the valley beyond are more meads, and oaks;   and, over these, far away, the sunny haze has thickened till the hills are a mere line. On the top of the right side of the valley is a clump of trees: from thence, from underneath, in a rocky cell, and at their very roots, rises a clear, cool spring. A rugged path, encumbered with brambles, winds down to it, to the bottom of the steep face of the stone where the water, with the moss-grown rock perpendicular to it, imperceptibly issues, with neither bubble nor sound. The fine sand of the shallow basin is still and undisturbed; no water-volcano thrusts up a dome of particles; nor is there any crevice or fissure piercing the stone. The basin is ever full and ever running over.

High above, the elms reach towards the sky, but a gleam of sunshine falls into the little pool: the sweet water emerges at once, from darkness into light. In a moment, it has slipped over the brim and found a descent where, severed into various threads, it rushes and winds to meet again as a streamlet covered in with water-cress and blue-flowered brook-lime, as if a green robe had been thrown over. But, still descending and growing, it presently flows   in the hollow of the valley,

where it has cut a deep channel, and scarce a quarter of a mile from its origin passes its first waggon-bridge.

In the old days, it seemed a journey from the apple tree here, down the golden mead, over the brook, beyond the thick stems of the marigolds, across the second streamlet, and so up the wild slope of the valley to the spring. The herbage there was short, and greyish, like a moor side; the earth in the hollow by the stream sank under the foot; the hollow oak and a few thorn bushes scattered apart, gave the feeling of a different and far away land. It was not fields: it was a moor.

I went to drink at the spring: the clear, cool, and sweet water tempted me in the summer. Stooping in the rocky cell, I lifted the water in the hollow of my hand, carefully else the sand might be disturbed. The sunlight gleamed on it as it slipped through my fingers; thus I had the sun, too, in my palm. Alone, under the roots of the trees and the step stone; alone, with the sunlight and the pure water, there was a sense of something more than these; the water was more to me than water; and the sun than sun—as if I had something in common with them and could feel with them. The gleaming ray on the liquid in my palm held me in its possession for the moment: the touch of the water gave me something from itself; it dropped from my fingers and was gone; the gleam disappeared, but I had had them. Beside the physical water and the physical light, my soul had received from them their beauty.*

The sun shone and I said: Give me more life, I held out my palm to hold the sunlight like water. Let me be filled with the life of light as my hand is filled with water when I dip from the brook.

* See a similar passage in "Meadow Thoughts".

The Buttercups: From the Tree to the Pool

In those days I carried home some   water from the spring—in a tin can, plainest of vessels—merely to drink it again in the garden. There was plenty of water there (pumps to which the hamlet came), and the brook, too, close by.   But this was different; this was from the spring: pure, crystal, and holy in its truth to itself; it was brought home as a beautiful flower might be brought.

This valley of the spring and the hollow oak lies quiet: the place of utter peace, under the sun—as he rises higher, the horses on the distant slope go to the trees, and the valley itself recedes. It appears farther away as the air lit with glowing beams makes its presence known to the eyes without being actually seen.

The russet apple gives no shelter to the seat, and it must be left for a time   till the evening is near. Still, I can think elsewhere while the meadow burns with gold under the noonday sun. These buttercups have no number, scale or place. The slope, the furrow, the level: they are everywhere, growing as they fancy. There are no rows, or lines, or banks, or parallels, or places more thickly sown to give a heavier mass of colour.   No relief of white, or green, or blue: the lesser flowers are quite hidden, and the grass concealed, for the branches of the buttercups twine so that it looks an unbroken surface of yellow. Neither does the colour change to meet the changing sky: it is always yellow under the rain, the lightning, the moonlight, the dawn. A fixed yellow: the same this year, last year, and the next; no variation to charm us, to make us watch for the opening blossom in expectation of something new. The colour, then, is not especially for me. I admire it; so vividly is it impressed upon my memory that in the midst of winter and sunless snow I can see the brilliant meadow as plainly as if I stood up to my knees in the summer grass. But I should have admired it equally, I know, if it had been violet or purple instead of gold, and I feel that if I (or the whole of the human race) were extinct the colour would be the same. The buttercup would open its petal to the sun just the same if I did not exist: I am nothing to it. Thousands upon thousands, no doubt, in the old times, did so open their petals and were never seen by man. It was nothing to them. Nor do they grow in any position to please me: this particular meadow is full of them, but only just over the bank there are scarcely any; nor do they sow themselves in mathematical lines to please my idea of proportion. They set me and my ideas of proportion utterly at variance. They grow anyhow, and their colour is for them and not for me; they scatter themselves, a chaos of brilliance along the sward. They are entirely useless. Nothing eats them; if they are not cut down by the scythe they stay till the autumn winds bleach and over-throw them. No creature uses them as food: they are so intensely bitter. You could not, probably, eat enough of the root, so acrid is it; but, if you could, it would kill you with acrid bitterness. Golden glory above, poisonous bitterness below. Yet they yield no medicinal or healing essence which could not be obtained from other plants.

The buttercup is superfluous to man: he could exist if the last were exterminated; just as the buttercup could live if he were non-existent. There is no link between them. The butterflies pass them: the bees go by; some few flies perhaps alight here and there; if there were no buttercups, they would alight on something else. I doubt whether, if no buttercups sprang up next spring, any living creature would be a jot the loser.

The drift of my thought would be unaltered if someone declared that a certain insect is dependent on the buttercup, for we ourselves depend upon the plant

wheat (which is nothing but grass); yet I do not think that the grass, wheat, is any more specially existent for man's food than the colour of the buttercup for my admiration. The buttercups extend where man never saw them; the grass, wheat, existed, in all probability, many ages before its seed was used. If man fell out of existence to-morrow, the grass, wheat, would continue just the same as the grass which the horses eat.

The buttercups know nothing of man: neither does the grass whose seed maintains him. We sow the wheat in a line, but it never so sowed itself; nor do the buttercups. Wheat is the most useful, not only to us but to innumerable birds: buttercups the most useless; but they are both exactly on a level—both plants.

Poison, the deadly nightshade, is not existent to poison us; nor wheat to feed us; nor buttercups because they are harmlessly useless.

OHC–D

Chapter 7

ABSENCE OF DESIGN IN NATURE

IN the parlour to which I have retired from the heat there is a chair and a table, and a picture on the wall: the chair was made for an object and a purpose, to sit in; the table for a purpose, to write on; the picture was painted for a purpose, to please the eye. But outside, in the meadow, in the hedge, on the hill, in the water; or, looking still farther, to the sun, the moon, and stars, I see no such chair, or table, or picture.

Pondering deeply and for long upon the plants, the living things (myself, too, as a physical being): upon the elements, on the holy miracle, water; the holy miracle, sunlight; the earth, and the air, I come at last —and not without, for a while, sorrow—to the inevitable conclusion that there is no object, no end, no purpose, no design, and no plan; no anything, that is.

By a strong and continued effort, I compelled myself to see the world mentally: with my mind, as it were, abstracted; hold yourself, as it were, apart from it, and there is no object, and no plan; no law, and no rule.

From childhood we build up for ourselves an encyclopædia of the world, answering all questions: we turn to Day, and the reply is Light; to Night, and the reply is Darkness. It is difficult to burst through these fetters and to get beyond Day and Night: but, in truth, there is no Day and Night; the sun always shines. It is our minds which supply the purpose, the end, the plan, the law, and the rule. For the practical matters of life, these are sufficient—they are like conventional agreements. But if you wish to really know the truth, there is none. When you first realize this, the whole arch of thought falls in; the structure the brain has reared, or, rather, which so many minds have reared for it, becomes a crumbling ruin, and there seems nothing left. I felt crushed when I first saw that there was no chair, no table, no picture, in nature: I use "nature" in the widest sense; in the cosmos then. Nothing especially made for man to sit on, to write on, to admire—not even the colour of the buttercups or the beautiful sun-gleam which had me spellbound glowing on the water in my hand in the rocky cell.

The rudest quern ever yet discovered in which the earliest man ground his wheat did not fall from the sky; even that poor instrument, the mere hollowed stone, was not thrown to him prepared for use; he had to make it himself. There neither is, nor has been, nor will be any chair, or table, or picture, or quern in the cosmos. Nor is there any plan even in the buttercups themselves, looked at for themselves: they are not geometrical, or mathematical; nor precisely circular, nor anything regular. A general pattern, as a common colour, may be claimed for them, a pattern, however, liable to modification under cultivation; but, fully admitting this, it is no more than saying that water is water: that one crystal is always an octahedron,* another a dodecahedron;† that one element is oxygen and another hydrogen; that the earth is the earth; and the sun, the sun. It is only stating in the simplest way

* Solid figure contained by eight plane faces.
† Solid figure of twelve faces.

the fact that a thing *is*:   and, after the most rigid research, that is, in the end, all that can be stated.

To say that there is a general buttercup pattern is only saying that it is not a bluebell or violet. Perhaps the general form of the buttercup is not absolutely necessary to its existence; many birds can fly equally well if their tails be removed, or even a great part of their wings. There are some birds that do not fly at all. Some further illustrations presently will arise; indeed, nothing could be examined without affording some. I had forgotten that the parlour, beside the chair and table, had a carpet. The carpet has a pattern: it is woven; the threads can be discerned, and a little investigation shows beyond doubt that it was designed and made by a man. It is certainly pretty and ingenious. But the grass of my golden meadow has no design, and no purpose: it is beautiful, and more; it is divine.

When at last I had disabused my mind of the enormous imposture of a design, an object, and an end, a purpose or a system, I began to see dimly how much more grandeur, beauty and hope there is in a divine chaos—not chaos in the sense of disorder or confusion but simply the absence of order—than there is in a universe made by pattern. This draught-board universe my mind had laid out: this machine-made world and piece of mechanism; what a petty, despicable, microcosmus I had substituted for the reality.

Logically, that which has a design or a purpose has a limit. The very idea of a design or a purpose has since grown repulsive to me, on account of its littleness. I do not venture, for a moment, even to attempt to supply a reason to take the place of the exploded plan. I simply deliberately deny, or, rather, I have now advanced to that stage that to my own mind even the admission of the subject to discussion is impossible. I look at the sunshine and feel that there is no contracted order: there is divine chaos, and, in it, limitless hope and possibilities.

Chapter 8

THE PRODIGALITY OF NATURE AND NIGGARDLINESS OF MAN

WITHOUT number, the buttercups crowd the mead: not one here and there, or sufficient only to tint the sward. There is not just enough for some purpose: there they are without number, in all the extravagance of uselessness and beauty. The apple-bloom—it is falling fast now as the days advance—who can count the myriad blossoms of the orchard? There are leaves upon the hedges which bound that single meadow on three sides (the fourth being enclosed by a brook) enough to occupy the whole summer to count; and before it was half done they would be falling. But that half would be enough for shadow—for use.

Half the rain that falls would be enough. Half the acorns on the oaks in autumn, more than enough. Wheat itself is often thrown into the sty. Famines and droughts occur, but whenever any comes it is in abundance—sow a grain of wheat, and the stalk, one stalk alone, of those that rise from it will yield forty times.

There is no *enough* in nature. It is one vast prodigality. It is a feast. There is no economy: it is all one immense extravagance. It is all giving, giving, giving: no saving, no penury; a golden shower of good things is for ever descending. I love beyond all things to contemplate this indescribable lavishness—I would it could be introduced into our human life. I know, none better, having gone through the personal experience myself, that it is at the present moment impossible to practise it: that each individual is compelled, in order to exist, to labour, to save, and to economize. I know, of course, as all do who have ever read a book, that attempts to distribute possessions, to live in community of goods, have each failed miserably. If I rightly judge, the human race would require a century of training before even an approximation to such a thing were possible. All this, and much more to the same effect, I fully admit. But still the feeling remains and will not be denied. I dislike the word economy: I detest the word thrift; I hate the thought of saving. Maybe some scheme in the future may be devised whereby such efforts may be turned to a general end. This alone I am certain of: there is no economy, thrift, or saving, in nature; it is one splendid waste. It is that waste which makes it so beautiful, and so irresistible! Now nature was not made by man, and is a better exemplar than he can furnish: each thread in this carpet goes to form the pattern; but go out into my golden mead and gather ten thousand blades of grass, and it will not destroy it.

Perhaps there never were so many houses upon the face of the earth as at the present day: so luxuriously appointed, so comfortable, so handsomely furnished. Yet, with all this wealth and magnificence, these appointments and engineering: with all these many courses at dinner and array of wines, it has ever seemed to me a mean and penurious age. It is formal and in order; there is no heart in it. Food should be broadcast, open, free: wine should be in flagons, not in tiny glasses; in a word, there should be genial waste. Let the crumbs fall: there are birds enough to pick them up.

The Old House at Coate

The greatest proof of the extreme meanness of the age is the long list of names appended to a subscription for a famine or a fashionable charity. Worthy as are these objects, the donors write down their own unutterable meanness. There are men in their warehouses, their offices, on their lands, who have served them honourably for years and have received for their wage just exactly as much as experience has proved can be made to support life. No cheque with a great flourishing signature has ever been presented to them.

I say that the entire labouring population—some skilled trades excepted as not really labouring—is miserably underpaid, not because there is a pressure or scarcity, a trouble, a famine, but from pure selfishness. This selfishness, moreover, is not intentional, but quite unconscious; and individuals are not individually guilty, because they are within their rights. A man has a hundred thousand pounds: he eats and drinks and pleases his little whims—likely enough quite innocent little whims—but he never gives to a friend, or a relation; never assists, does nothing with it. This is commercially right, but it is not the buttercups in the golden mead; it is not the grain of wheat that yielded forty times. It is not according to the exemplar of nature. Therefore I say that although I admit all attempts to adjust possessions have been and for the age at least must prove failures, yet my feeling remains the same. Thrift, economy, accumulation of wealth, are inventions; they are not nature. As there are more than enough buttercups in this single meadow for the pleasure of all the children in the hamlet, so too it is a fact, a very stubborn fact, that there is more than enough food in the world for all its human children. In the year 1880, it was found, on careful calculation made for strictly commercial purposes, that there was a surplus grain production of* bushels. That is to say, if every buttercup in this meadow represented a bushel of wheat, there would be all that over and above what was necessary. This is a very extraordinary fact. That the wheat has to be produced, to be distributed; that there are a thousand   social complications to be considered, is, of course, incontrovertible. Still, there was the surplus; bushels of golden grain as numerous as the golden buttercups.

But that does not represent the capacity of the earth for production: it is not possible to gauge that capacity —so practically inexhaustible is it.

Thrift and economy and accumulation, therefore, represent a state of things contrary to the exemplar of nature, and in individual life they destroy its beauty. There is no pleasure without waste: the banquet is a formality; the wine tasteless, unless the viands and the liquor are in prodigal quantities. Give me the lavish extravagance of the golden mead!

* There is a blank in the manuscript here.

Chapter 9

AERIAL NAVIGATION AND THE FLIGHT OF
BIRDS AND INSECTS

I

IN the very early morning, while the house was yet still, although fully lit up by the sun, sleeping in broad daylight, a thrush used to come to the wooden seat under the russet apple. There he would perch and look well round him, wait a minute or two, and listen to see that no one was moving, and then go across to the strawberries which grew under the parlour window. He was sure to find something there. Often while sitting, thinking, in the old oak chair, I have heard a slight

rustling and knew it was a thrush under the window-sill. The strawberries grew up to the wall; by raising the window they could be gathered from the room. Occasionally a thrush would chip a snail on the seat under the russet: so, in the hedges where an elm or oak has been sawn off and the butt left in the ground, they bring their prey to batter the shell to fragments on the hard level wood.

There was a low box hedge along the top of the ha-ha, only the breadth of the stones between it and the hedge, but that breadth was fully occupied with wall grasses and moss. To these, many birds came, later on, for seeds; the grasses decayed and were bleached by wind and sun, forming a grey fringe outside the dull green box. This was the insects' jungle: moths and butterflies, and many winged creatures which have no English name, curiously coloured, with wings veined like a translucent leaf, come to sun themselves. The wild bees visited it by day: at dusk, white moths. It was the place to watch for a hornet—not that he stayed, but went by, with formidable hum, to the orchard. The yellow streaked bees which hover in one spot for a few seconds, and then dart to another a yard distant, agitate their wings with such velocity that the body of the insect alone appears: the wings, if you see them, are like a faint cloud around it, no more tangible than the air lit by the sun, which is visible and yet cannot be seen. This extreme speed has induced me to imagine that the insect is unconscious of the action of its vanes.

As the engineer touches a valve and immediately the wheels revolve, yet when whirling at their highest speed he does not feel any exertion, so the insect having admitted by conscious will the vital force to the machinery of its flight has no further effort, no more than we have to maintain the beating of the pulse.

In such a matter there is at present nothing further than conjecture; still, I cannot but think that flight is no effort whatever; that it involves nothing like what we call muscular exertion, such as we feel in walking or turning a handle.

An insect never gives the impression of weariness, or of exertion. At night, the coolness, and perhaps the absence or quiescence of the subtle electric, or whatever name is correctly given to the force of life, causes many insects to become almost helpless. They do not seem tired, but simply like a mechanism without its motive force; like a spent bullet without the impulse of the explosion; like a dropped leaf which the wind no longer whirls. The rays of the sun warm them; the action of the zoistic electricity re-commences, and they buzz across the fields, traversing distances which, in comparison with their own size are immense, without the least apparent effort.

It is quite different with their legs and feet: the effort of moving some slight particle, of climbing, of the bee opening the petals of a flower, is evident. The thing is not open to proof or disproof. I would merely say it is my feeling that the bee travels without conscious effort. The horse knows when each hoof comes down; the bee's wing swings round disconnected with its mind, and it does not recognize what part of the arc it is at the moment transcribing. This apparent separation of the nerve, of the brain, from the mechanism, gave me the idea of constructing an insect. When the motion, as in the horse, originates in the mind, and is always in communication with it, the action is clearly so delicate and subtle that to make anything resembling it, even rudely, is at present almost beyond attempt, though not so in the future.

But if my conjecture be in a measure correct: that the insect's wings rotate without its conscious exertion, there seems a possibility of tracing the manner of its movement. That part, then, of the insect I propose for imitative construction is the mechanical. The dry, fleshless, frame of the insect resembles a machine far more than the substance of the animal limb which feels. The animal limb has something more than muscle, sinew, nerve, and the apparatus of motion: the mind is in constant connexion with every single atom of its surface. In comparison, the insect resembles a tubular frame.

I have no doubt insects have minds, but I am now looking at their physical and outward structure. They themselves possess thought and feeling: but their outward structure is more, or appears more, mechanical; and, so far as the wings are concerned, to be driven very much independent of their consciousness. Could the condition be imitated; could saccharine be decomposed (as they seem, or many of them, to live on sugar), under the same chemical conditions, may it not be imagined that the electric force would play its part and exert its force, and that if the mechanism were connected motion would take place without feeling or consciousness?

Possibly a motor may be worked out from the insect's wing: possibly it may assist in solving the problems, afford a means of aerial navigation. One difficulty of that navigation is the lack of an engine at once light enough, capable of working on very little fuel, and at immense speed. The insect answers all these.

Perhaps the dragon-fly would be the best model for the external shape of an airship: the wing cases representing the inclined plane, the tail enabling it to manœuvre with singular dexterity. The insect requires but minute fuel: when the sugar congeals, as the dew falls, its fuel will not burn.

I write "a means of aerial navigation" because I think in all probability several methods of flying will almost simultaneously be discovered. The idea of constructing

an engine to work like the insect has occupied me a long time. From the seat under the russet apple tree too, the flight of swallows as they skimmed just above the buttercups; of blackbirds to and fro the hedges and the brook; of woodpigeons passing higher in the air; of rooks, hawks at times, and incessantly of starlings, could be observed. The starlings, having nests in the thatch by the chimney, were to and fro all day long, and the action of their wings could be minutely observed: rapid flight to easy motion; floating; turning; the way in which balance was recovered when one wing was higher than the other, the body leaning to one side; how the wing when extended was almost transparent, the feathers, as it were, so stretched apart, and that fringe, but just touching so that the light was just visible through. Their manner of starting from the perch I saw clearly from my bedroom window: they often perched on an iron bar that projected there to hold the window open, and by approaching the window carefully I used to admire the play of iridescence, green, gold, blue, black, and bronze, on their folded wings. A slight movement was enough to make the bird start like a skater from the bar, throwing himself upon the abyss of the air, the jerk of the start causing the iron bar to quiver and emit a low musical note.

When writing or reading in that room, I knew by the sound of the vibrating metal every time a bird had sprung from it. Entering into the being of the bird, and feeling with it, which I could not help doing from continued observation, it seemed to me that flight ' cost it little exertion. I came to the conclusion that it was much less effort for it to fly than for me to run. There was no expense of vast muscular strength, no blow or forcible impression upon the air like a sledge upon the anvil. The actual mechanism of flight was fragile in the extreme: the actual expenditure of force at any given moment extremely minute. This, of course, refers to birds that really fly, and not to those that pass great part of their time on foot, or floating. The merest touch of the wing was sufficient, the merest gentle fanning. To continue that fanning for twenty hours at a stretch, which is what the swallow and swift can easily accomplish, needs no doubt greater engine power, as it were, or the means of constantly replenishing animal heat—in fact, the fuel—by food: which either of these birds can do, as they take their food on the wing and find it in the air: or both these conditions.

Nothing, therefore, that I now put forth is incompatible with the existence of large muscles in the bird: I am referring to the movement of flight, the beat of the wing, the actual action which causes suspension in the air. Suspension and forward motion is, I think, accomplished (not without conscious effort as in insects) with conscious effort, but with such ease, such gentle fanning and mere touch upon the air, that it is difficult to convey an idea of the delicacy of the stroke.

Each species of bird has a mannerism of flight by which it can be distinguished at long distances: some use their wings quickly, as starlings; others, slow and with short pauses; some rise and fall, like the finches; but probably the influence of their wings upon the air is the same. The rook is one of the best to watch, because, being so numerous, every variation is seen, and as he flies slow the position of the wings is visible throughout their stroke. He strolls through the air. You can count the vibrations of his wings: he uses them so faintly and with such dilettante disdain of labour that the air seems rather to spread his feathers for him than he to fly for himself. Neither rapid iteration, sharp percussion, nor length of reach is necessary. His vanes scarce describe two-thirds the arc of which they are capable: they do not hit the air downwards but softly press it as he glides; after the stroke they recover position gently. It is the more remarkable because he is able to do all these: to strike the air; to reiterate the blow swiftly; to stretch his wing; if fear, haste, or strong winds necessitate exertion. Simply to fly is nothing to him. The air spreads his feathers for him, and the form of undulatory motion may enable us to fly. The supporting power of the air when, as it were, enclosed in folds and moving in a wave may be demonstrated by simple experiments: a sheet of thin paper held at the edge and vibrated; and, far better, a sheet or table-cloth. As the housemaid spreads the cloth she lifts the edge by

her hand and the vane of air rolls along between it and the surface of the table. Possibly an undulating wing may be devised: a fan held by its centre and vibrating along its length forming the air into vanes and grasping it.

2

In swimming, it has been discovered that the forward motion is derived from the legs thrusting a wedge of water backwards: they are kicked out apart and then come together; and the wedge of water between is squeezed backwards, causing the swimmer to advance. The wings of a bird act as they fold, in the same manner: driving a wedge of air behind them; and they use gravitation, the power which pulls downwards, as an aid, and a great one, to their progress, for they are always balanced and sliding. So far as advance is concerned, the existence of gravitation is an advantage to them, for they use it to pull them along.

Besides, however, these mechanical or physical means, there is in the bird one yet more important factor of flight: and that is, consciousness, and life, that subtle power for which no accurate term has been selected, the *desire* to go forward, and the effort which makes every feather instinct with energy.

A swift skater conceives the will to turn, and immediately, without special effort, he turns: there is a connexion between the will and the steel bound to the foot. The bird desires to fly, to rise or turn, and the will-power, in some subtle manner, adjusts its mere mechanical means to the air. Those mechanical means, the beautifully formed feathers, the expanding wing, might perhaps, if only worked by some inanimate power like

electricity, fail of effort. The desire and will to go forward would be lacking. That will was visible in the
starling as he sprang from the trembling iron catch of
the window: you may see it in the rook suddenly increasing his idle stroll as he perceives his friends feast-
ing; in the finch, rising and falling as he flies. The stroke
of his little wings, so quickly folded, is accompanied by
an evident throw of his body forward: the will in him,
like an afflatus, carries him along.

This must necessarily be absent from any machine,
however cunningly constructed. It is absent, or nearly,
as just now observed, from the flight of many insects
which fly by machinery; by the swift rotation of a
screw as it were, machinery which instantly obeys their
will but is not inspired by it. The wing of the insect
seems to compel the air by sheer rapidity of stroke: the
wing of the rook seems spread by the air itself.

From all these observations I draw the assured con-
viction that aerial navigation is a certainty of the future.
The rook demonstrated that flight needs no immense
exertion: that the wing need not strike the air with
extraordinary force, or with incalculable velocity of
repetition; that its area need not of necessity be large.
Three-fourths of the difficulties in the way of the
mechanician are thus swept aside—he has not to set out
to construct a machine delivering enormous power or
speed exercised over a vast expanse. If I understand the
motion of the wind aright, it is not at all beyond the
reach of skill to imitate. Man has sufficient muscular
power to work wings proportionately equal in size to
those of the rook, for it must be borne in mind that his
strength is not confined to the arms only, but legs can
treble his force when pressing a treadle. His flight by his

unaided personal powers ought, I think, to extend, under favourable conditions, to one hundred miles. The tenuity of the air permits anything to pass through it with so little friction that with no wind still a speed of twenty or twenty-five an hour might be calculated upon; and this a man in a fair physical state might maintain, as he could carry some slight refreshment with him, for at least four or five hours. I think this is a moderate estimate.

I see nothing in the idea of such flight at all comparable with the heroic feat of swimming the Channel.* The herculean power of muscle, the enduring vigour, the resistance to cold, the whole physical force employed; and, last but not least, the will-force which could withstand the extreme monotony of stroke after stroke, so many thousand repetitions, far, far exceeds anything required for flight.

As a swimmer from early youth, I can thoroughly appreciate the immense power displayed. To me, the greatest difficulty of a long swim was always the monotony, the ceaseless iteration of the same motion making so little progress for each individual effort. But think of this for forty interminable miles! Since the world's history began to be written there is no record of such a feat: all the heroes of antiquity never achieved anything approaching it; not even Grecian imagination endowed its mythic heroes with such endurance—for even Ulysses was supported by the gift of a nymph in the sea. Homer could not conceive of his doing it unaided.

To me, this marvellous swim was a great triumph, for it has always been a favourite supposition of mine

* By Captain Webb.

Aerial Navigation, Flight of Birds and Insects

that man is capable of exceeding all animals in physical endurance. I say with deliberation that the feat of swimming the Channel so far exceeds the effort of flight on the part of a bird that no comparison is possible. Furnish a man of that physique with wings, and he could work them with ease. A hundred miles at a stretch is a most moderate estimate. A man who could swim forty miles through so inelastic a medium as sea, against wind, wave, current, cold, exposure, could, in my opinion, if furnished with wings like those of the swift, fly through the thin and yielding air ten times as far and alight rather four hundred than one hundred miles distant.

Those who talk of the muscular power of the bird, of the immense force of the wing, in a tone of hopelessness at man's incapability, simply reveal their narrowness of view. I say that the bird is a weak and feeble creature, compared with man, and deliberately affirm from most careful observation that man is perfectly capable of extended flight. Give him the wings, enable him to apply the real strength of his body, and he will do it.

The greatest power of the human body seems to be exercised downwards, while standing, through the feet: imagine a yoke on your shoulder, to push against, your body ever so slightly bent, and your feet pressing something. Perhaps the treadle, or some modification of it, may ultimately afford the connexion.

For the conveyance of heavy materials, or quiescent passengers, anything beyond man himself, no doubt some form of vessel will be needed; and then I am not so sure that the bird's wing offers the best model. The insect's wing, whose effect depends on rapid rotation, is possibly more likely to lead to some invention. The bird's wing wants the will, and ceaseless adjustment to the varying air; the insect's wing revolves like machinery, the same whether the wind blow high or low, and does not apparently require adjustment. Hence, for a machine not intimately directed by man's will, perhaps the insect's wing—some form of screw—presents the best natural model. Here, the one great want is the motor: some light engine requiring little fuel or water. It may be that some method of stored force may accomplish this: instead of carrying engine, boiler, coal, and water, it is just possible that the boiler, the coal and water, may impart their energy to the engine, and that the latter, detached, may work the vessel.

Imagine a Leyden jar then, with stored electricity, driving the vanes of an aerial ship till its contents were exhausted, when its place could be supplied by another.

What has chiefly hindered progress in the arts and sciences, and indeed in all things, is the dogmatic assumption that this or that cannot be done, that it is impossible, till thousands of minds—nay, even whole generations—view the idea of an attempt as an impious violation of that flagrant falsehood which for ages smothered the soul, i.e., the assertion that man and his mind are finite. The assumption has been that we do not possess sufficient physical power to work wings, even if invented. This assumption I utterly deny and repudiate. We *do* possess ample physical power to work wings.

Chapter 10

THE WALL BELOW THE APPLE TREE

I

THE wall of the ha-ha below the russet apple was not without its colour: grey lichen; moss, bright green in autumn, in summer, pale and dry; spots of red velvet, where butterflies settled and spread their wings; blue specks, where lesser butterflies alighted on the drooping grass along the summit; dragon-flies rushing to and fro; often a blue tit, whose nest was in a cranny, or who came that way with an eye to the hive bees. His nest was never on this face of the wall, the western, but always on the other which faced the south, but he frequently came here. A brown wren

passed still more often: thus there was colour, but it was a minute study, the colour of detail.

The hedge between the Fern Close and the Brook Field—the buttercup mead—came to the ha-ha, joining it by some dry fence, as bushes will never grow quite close up to a wall or a tree. This dry fence, willow interwoven, over-shadowed by a young evergreen or holm oak bush which grew at an angle of the wall, was a robin's possession. The dead branch of an ash at the extremity of the hedge there belonged to a fly-catcher: all the summer long he sat there, flying three or four yards every other minute out over the grass, snapping an insect and returning.

THE COUNTRY NEAR LONDON

Chapter 1

THE SEASONS IN SURREY:
TREE AND BIRD LIFE IN THE COPSE

EARLY one morning in March, awaking as the
workmen's trains went rumbling by to the City,
I saw on the ceiling by the window a streak of sunlight, tinted orange and crimson by the vapour
through which the level beams had passed. The disk
had risen, as seen from here, almost over the metropolis,
illuminating with equal light the golden cross of St.
Paul's and the golden grasshopper of the Exchange.

There is something in the sense of morning which
lifts the heart with the sun. The light, the air, the
waving branches, speak: the mind, clear as if born
afresh, advances to meet them, full of joy and hope;
the earth and life seem boundless at that moment. It is
the same, I find, on the verge of the artificial city, as
where the rays come streaming from the Downs. It is
the same light, the same morning, and not all the
offices, warehouses, the materialistic tone of common
conversation (a very decided trait of London life) can
efface the feeling of something holy in the sunrise. For
the moment, the morning makes the earth a temple.

While I thus thought, looking at the streak of sunshine, suddenly there rang out three clear trumpet-like
notes from a tree at the end of a little copse near the
garden. A softer song followed, and then again the
same three notes whose wild sweetness echoed through
the trees. It was a missel-thrush, the stormcock and
trumpeter of spring. His voice sounded not only close

at hand but seemed to again repeat itself as it went away, as a bugle does. Lord of March, his proud call challenges the woods: there are none who can compare with him. Listen for the missel-thrush: when he sings, the snow may drift, the rain fall, but not for long; the violets are near at hand.

Next, a tiny chiff-chaff called from the top of a tall birch, and scarcely had he gone on than a titmouse began, but, busy as he was, he could not visit all the myriad buds around him. From a pine, greenfinches went by, talking to each other; a yellow-hammer called, but with shortened notes; and a lark (he had been up long since) arose again, singing, from the thin mist over the surface of an arable field by the copse. Starlings came to the spouting of the roof, whistling eagerly, full of the approaching business of nesting: how excited they get!

The sunbeam on the ceiling descended down the wall, losing the crimson and orange, and growing white as the disk left the vapour of the horizon and shone undimmed in the blue sky.

Blackbirds uttered low whistles in several differing directions. With the chirping of sparrows, the "fink" of chaffinches, the "caw, caw" of rooks, floating over, the day opened. And, day by day, looking from my window up the field beside the copse there appeared some new, slight change, some sign that the invisible forces of the sun were working here, too, as afar. The slender, drooping, birch boughs, which once reflected the light as if each twig were polished, were now thickening with opening buds. In the elms there was a reddish mist: the wind had a different sound in the trees; no longer the hollow whistle of bare branches, the

network was growing and held the breeze. Near at hand,
a larch was already touched with the tenderest green:
the boughs of a horse-chestnut close by were enlarged
at the tip where the buds were bursting. To the holly
bush adjacent, though within half gunshot, a fieldfare,
even the wild and untamable fieldfare, resorted for the
berries in the terrible frosts of January 1880, driven by
hunger almost to the door.

The glance can still penetrate some distance into the
copse: but the woodbine, its green slightly tinted with
dull purple, is covering the poles to which it clings.
Along the enclosing hedge there runs a straggling and
uncertain line of green; hawthorn and brier, the docks
and nettles and parsley of the mound, each add their
part. The ploughed field is losing its brown, the innumerable blades that are springing up hiding the
clods; but as they were not planted by nature, but by
mechanical art, with regular spaces between, they do
not yet entirely conceal the ground. The very heaps of
rubbish in the corner and by the gateway are disappear-
ing under green: weeds, if you like, but still green. The
meadows on the slope almost a mile away have a much
more vivid hue than a short while since. Upon one
short oak in the hedgerow this side of them the leaves
of last year adhere; its brown foliage is thrown out in
contrast with the sward behind, and the faint green of a
hawthorn bush whose lines are appearing beside it.
There are spots of yellow among the furze; it will be
one breadth of golden bloom shortly. Yonder, in the
arable plain, white puffs of steam drift before the east
wind, which dissipates it almost as quickly as it issues
from the funnel of the ploughing engine. The sunshine
gleams on polished brass; the black boiler and huge dull

red wheels stand out clearly against the brown of the soil. These men are at work with the first note of the thrush; they cease only with the darkness. A clear blue sky extends overhead, without a cloud, but it is of a hard tint—March blue—and the furrows yonder, fresh-turned, must whiten and crumble quickly under the dry air.

The first swallow is usually seen near about the same spot every year: in this district, the first is generally noticed by some farm buildings where there is a large pond. The swifts, too, are often noted first in the same old locality, over the open country; the bats, likewise, up and down the same road in the evening. The cuckoo, again, calls first from the same direction, and always at a distance; never do you hear the cuckoo, first, close at hand; and the first nightingale sings in the same old mound.

Thus, too, with flowers: the lesser celandine, the marsh marigold, the violets, all appear earlier in one spot than in others: the silvery cuckoo-flower or lady-smock offers itself by one particular furrow first.

Knowing these places, one can observe or hear the birds, and gather the flowers, long before most people have even thought of looking or listening. In this little copse there has been a missel-thrush's nest every season I have known it, always in the birches and never far from the same spot. Probably the birds built there generations (thrush generations) before I knew it.

Birches grow in a curious and uncertain fashion: the trunk twists upon its base and, instead of a circular stem, presents irregular rounded angles and longitudinal grooves; besides which there are often hollows and cavities where branches have decayed. On such ledges, or where a large bough joins the trunk, the missel-thrush builds his nest.

The last note I listen for in the copse is that of the turtle-dove. It always comes from the same spot, but it is often, as it seems, long delayed. The dove is not hasty: he does not woo till the soft showers have fallen and the raindrops have glittered on the green leaves. Then, some morning, just as I have said to myself he will not come this year, some injury has befallen him, the soft "coo, coo" murmurs forth from among the trees, and I know that spring is really here.

Wood-pigeons call occasionally in the copse all the warmer season through; in winter a flock of them visit it. Jays scream and flutter round the tree-tops; magpies very rarely come, though there are plenty close at hand; or woodpeckers. There are rabbits, both there and in some furze adjacent, but not many—the stray cats are too numerous. There are pheasants, too; sometimes I

can see one running beside the hedge of the copse—a pheasant does not run straight but in a series of sidelong motions, tracing a winding line; twice I have seen them within gunshot. As there is no preservation, properly speaking, they must come from preserves at some distance. Pheasants will never learn to stay at home....*

The wagtails keep within earshot, chirping almost day and night, about some small ponds among the furze. To appearance, the little stream is much more suitable to their habits, but birds are far from always acting as advantage would seem to direct. They have their likes and dislikes, their fancies, the same as creatures of larger make.

Nightingales, in the same manner, keep away from this copse, yet build in the adjacent furze. The robins have each their own especial demesne, a little district around this tree. One has his favourite perch on the wooden railings crossing the streamlet where it flows out through the hedge. If a wagtail dares to visit the sandy shore of the little brook just there, the robin is instantly on the spot and drives him away by force of arms.

Glass is a great difficulty to most creatures: they only understand it after experience. I saw a robin, one winter day, here, trying time after time to get through the fanlight over a hall door. He was probably a bird of the year: he returned to the glass again and again till he had convinced himself it was impossible to enter.

A barn or white owl frequently goes round the copse in the evening: if not seen, his screech may be heard. Cuckoos are very fond of it; there is almost always one about it during the months they are in this country. As for the thrushes and blackbirds, they are always to be heard in the season of song. Whitethroats, too, are numerous: but blackcaps rather rare: wrynecks travel past, but do not seem to stay—they appear to

* P. 10 of manuscript is missing.

have a partiality for some extensive orchards not far distant.

This small copse, which can be easily seen through, so soon as the leaves begin to fall, is bounded on two sides by highway roads along which there is a heavy traffic: it is within the London delivery of goods and the vans and carts of well-known tradesmen pass it daily; it is scoured by boys and people picking up dead sticks (though nominally private, such folk, of course, will go in); and yet, notwithstanding these drawbacks, it is a favourite resort of all these and many other birds. If it could be kept quiet, without doubt game would soon increase in it: pheasants, as it is, periodically visit it. Anyone who watched it for a few days only in spring (when birds reveal their presence by their notes, often escaping notice at other times) would be convinced of the variety and abundance of bird and animal life near the metropolis.

When the declining autumn sun, fast drooping to the horizon, shines on the western side, on the oaks, beeches, birches, and maple bushes, buff and reddish orange, yellow and brown tints light up the vale, as it were, of the wood with such a beautiful breadth of colour that even the pre-occupied "city" man cannot but stay a minute to admire it.

Wild hops hang their grape-like vines along the bushes; white bryony tendrils coil along the hedges; honeysuckle clings and climbs; bittersweet opens its noisome flowers and hangs its red berries, which stay on the bines long after every leaf has dropped; celandine grows in the shady nooks; square stemmed figwort flourishes; in the streamlet water-parsnip grows and grows till its lengthening stems seem too much for the

81

roots and are swept away by the first freshet; June roses bloom and bramble bushes flower; by the footpaths, heath puts forth its bells; it is so much like the country with these old familiar things, and yet how widely different!

The plough travels to and fro, the wheat springs green, ripens and is reaped; the stubble, as I write to-day, is bleaching white beside the copse; these, too, are the same old familiar things.

There is an old shepherd who trudges by, with bent back, breeches and gaiters, stumping along with his stick, and his dog at his heels; with old-fashioned courtesy, if you meet him on the narrow footpath, he gives you the whole of the path and walks in the road to let you pass—the very antipodes, this, of the rude manners of the town.

The winter wind carries the snowflakes drifting against the copse, and every tree is streaked with a line of white. Or in the morning the branches are entirely hidden with rime, and the sun rises clear and golden in the sharp frosty air.

Again, the spring comes, the spruce firs are yellow at the tips of their graceful boughs, yellow with young needles. The nightingale sings and the cuckoo calls: the same familiar sounds, and yet it is not country. The sense of quiet peace is the one thing wanting.

Round a country farmhouse, the calm is often intense. The elms stand tall and still; the cattle graze noiselessly; the horses group themselves naturally, with artistic instinct, in the shadow; the rooks go past, but their caw is not a noise; the barndoor cock crows idly; the atmosphere is still.

But the air about the London copse is full of movement: the roll of vans; the tramp of feet; the boom of trains; and even when for a moment these are not heard, even then there is a feeling that something is coming. So that, although the nightingale sings and cuckoo cries, the rooks caw, the jays scream, and the wood-pigeons call, the copse is not like the old copses.

But southwards a faint blue line of hills is visible through the boughs in spring before the leaves have fully filled the trees. Beyond the fields, and the brown oak, the blue sky descends, losing its blue as it nears the earth, to an indistinct horizon formed of dim woods which mingle with the vaporous margin.

Sometimes, in the luxurious idle warmth of early summer, when the wind breathes sweetly and the sunshine acts like a delicious narcotic, the slumberous mind finds rest there in the possibilities of the distance. For the infinite and the future can alone give rest.

The gaze loses itself beyond in the haze and dimness where the woods and hills and sky gather together; the mind travels on into the sky space, and beyond, and still beyond. For a little while the restlessness of the very air is gone, the sounds silent, the knowledge that London is hard by, forgotten. But only for a little while. The great city places its finger upon the minute hand of the clock of life and forces with its pressure the pendulum to beat quicker.

You have never done: you can never say "I have finished." That is the difference between the London life and the country life. There, the plough completes the ploughing and stays. The rick is built and thatched, and it is left. Each day's work is finished in itself, and the men and the horses rest. Here, no sooner is the work over than another work begins; letters arrive, or the social struggle begins; you *must* go to the theatre, only because you must *not* keep still.

The countryman, having done the one thing he has determined to do that day, attempts nothing further; if it is summer, he sits out of doors and gossips. The city

man has no sooner finished one thing than he takes up another: the same in this with pleasure as with business. Thus, the ticking of the clock is hastened.

Southwards, as I have said, there is a faint blue line of hills, with something of the mystery of hills. But northwards, over the furze, when it grows dark, there is a long, low arch of light. In summer, it might be mistaken for the glow which accompanies the progress of the midnight sun. If streamers shot up from it, it would be recognized as the aurora borealis. As it is steady and does not flicker, it cannot be caused by a fire. This light is the reflection of London. When the sky is cloudless and the atmosphere clear, as after a dry north-east wind, the light is faint and low, and might be overlooked. Rain often blots it out altogether, and so does fog. But if there is a vapour in the air, not exactly cloud but a thickness, then it shines red and threatening. Once now and then it lifts itself higher and takes a dull orange tint. At intervals it assumes an alarming aspect. There then seem to be small fleecy clouds, possessed of great reflecting power, floating at a low altitude. These are lit up, sometimes with orange, and sometimes with crimson—a lurid glow as if London were burning. It seems as if the conflagration were rolling up rapidly, but, in the morning, lo! there is nothing to be seen but fields and trees, and yellow spots of bloom among the furze.

Chapter 2

THE LAST OF A LONDON TROUT

BY the side of the Hogsmill brook, between it and the lane leading to Worcester Park, there is a long withy-bed which is more resorted to by the sedge-birds or brook-sparrows than any other place I know. Generally it has been difficult to see them because the withy itself is, as a rule, in leaf when they come, and the innumerable wands hide them, while, below, the ground is covered with a thick growth of sedges and flags. Last year, however, the withy stoles were polled, so that this spring the boughs are short and small, and, as it happened, the dry winter and easterly winds so checked the sedges that they are hardly half their height, and the flags are thin and not much fuller. The sedge-birds, therefore, have but little cover and are rarely seen to such advantage. There must be fifteen or twenty in the osiers; one or two frequent the bushes fringing the garden by the moat; others haunt the scattered willows farther down the stream—one by the wooden bridge before you get to the mill. They sing so much they seem to hardly have time to feed. Coming gently, on the grass, or where the dust is thick and deadens the footstep, with the object of approaching one that is singing, suddenly another begins in the thin thorn hedge on a branch that could be touched with the walking-stick. Yet though so near he is not quite visible: he is partly concealed behind the fork of the branch, and this is a habit with the sedge-birds. They are not in the least timid and they chatter at your elbow, and yet are always partially hidden. If it is on a withy, they choose a spot where the rods cross or bunch, as it were, together; if in the sedges, though it seems as if you could push the bird out with your foot, he is behind the stalks. To place some obstruction between themselves and anyone passing is their custom. As the foliage is this spring so thin, however, it needs but a little dexterity in peering to get a view.

The brook-sparrow perches aside on a sloping willow rod and, slightly raising his head, chatters—turning his

bill from side to side. It is a very tiny bill, and his little eye looks out from under a yellowish streak. His song at first sounds nothing but chatter, but, upon listening longer, a scale may be found. . . .*

Soon many other of these birds begin to sing, they

* P. 35 of manuscript is missing.

keep it up all day and most of the night. If at all wakeful they must find it a wearisome iteration.

[On a warm spring morning when the sunshine pours in among the willows, and even the white dust of the road is brighter, bringing out the clear diffraction of the shadows, their lively chatter and quick motions form a pleasant running commentary on the low sound of the stream rolling round the curve.

A moorhen's* call comes from the hatch close by where the water of the moat joins the brook. Broad yellow petals of marsh marigold stand up high among the sedges rising from the greyish-green ground covered with a film of semi-dried swamp-grass. Here and there are lilac-tinted cuckoo-flowers drawn upon taller stalks than those that grow in the meadow. The black flowers of the sedges or the tips of their triangular stems are powdered with yellow pollen; dark green sword flags are beginning to spread their fans; but just across the road on the topmost twigs of the birch poles there are swallows twittering, singing in the tenderest tones to their loves.

From the oaks in the Orchis Meads, titlarks mount above the highest bough, and then descend sing, sing, singing to the cowslips among the grass.]†

A jay calls in the circular copse yonder; solitary rooks go over to their nests in the elms on the hill, and their slow shadow travels on the sward. Blackbirds whistle in the distance, high up among the boughs. A faint breeze rustles the dry sedges of last year in the ditch beside the hedge.

Leaning on the grey and lichen-hung rails by the

* Or water hen's.
† Passage in brackets; see "A London Trout" in *Nature Near London*.

brook below the withys, the current glides by—it is the water and the low sound that renders the place so idle: the sunbeams brood, the air is still; let us, too, stay.

A wild apple in bloom hangs over the brook: when the petals fall they will float away with the stream.

Yellow iris flowers here in June when midsummer comes—the iris loves a thunder shower. The flags in the brook grow in bunches rising from stalks (which the water-rats nibble); these branches are irregular in shape, and so close together as to appear to have no order. These are not the flags that flower; you might follow many a winding brook for miles and, though full everywhere of flags, choked with them in places, you would never see anything but the green grooved and pointed leaves. They seem to grow everywhere; there is not a stream without them. The iris is much more local: so much so that at home, where there were several brooks, every nook and corner of which was known to me, besides the ponds, there was but one place where the flowering flag could be found, and that was beside the least of all the brooks. There was only a small quantity of it, so that it was a pleasant surprise to me to find the iris growing so freely in this withy-bed beside the Hogsmill brook. It may be distinguished in a moment because the leaves, shooting from the same stalk, spread like a fan—flat, with their edges to each other—in the same way as, but on a much larger scale than, the azure fleur-de-luce in gardens.

There are dozens of flags here, in the marshy ground; they do not show much at present because the spring has been so dry, but by June, if some showers fall, they will prevent the glance from seeing in between the willow-stoles. The leaves rise fully three feet and a half, sometimes four, and the stalks on which the flowers come out stand up straight, equally high. The leaves are then as broad as sword blades, and of the same shape; the plant is one of the largest that grows wild, and in its full luxuriance recalls what is said of the vegetation in tropical swamps. The marsh here was aglow with its yellow hues at midsummer 1879.

It was the wettest spring in recollection; the rain descended day after day till at last we ceased even to look round the horizon for a break in the clouds. Still rain, rain, all through May and June; nothing but rain. No one could walk far in such weather, so that the gradual unfolding of plants was not observed. One day, the 29th June, however, in despite of the threatening sky, I came up the Ewell Road and turned down the lane to Worcester Park. The lane was then often under water for a hundred yards or more from the overflow of the Hogsmill, and I did not expect to get past. But halfway down something yellow caught my eye and, looking into the osier bed, it seemed quite alight with iris bloom. The large yellow petals were everywhere high above the sedge; there were dozens of the flowers together here: one yonder by itself, then two or three, then another bunch.

Along the hedge, pale green horse-tails lined the shore, for the marsh was a foot deep in dark water, which could only be seen by parting the stalks of the sedges. Sedge and flag grew so thick that everything was hidden but the yellow bloom above, which was inaccessible because of the flood. But farther down, just where the withy ends, there was a bunch of iris on the bank which there ran above the surface. Here I walked in among them: the sword leaves and the golden bloom

came up to my shoulder; it was a thicket of flower.

Had anyone speculated upon the possible conse-
quences of an immense downpour of rain continued for
months, he would probably have considered that such
excessive moisture would destroy the flowers and spoil
the appearance of the fields. The weight of the raindrops
alone would beat off the petals and the roots would be
soaked and weakened.

Yet never was there such floral beauty as in the spring
and early summer of that disastrous year. The iris has
been already mentioned. On the other side of the line
there are some open meadows rising gradually, divided
by posts and rails, and with small copses, hawthorn
trees, and isolated oaks scattered about them. These are
very pleasant meadows, and over the slope there is a
birch wood, or larger copse. The low hedge by the lane
is always full of sedges; the dry leaves of last year's rise
high up among the thorns; the green stalks of these
push up beside them. Rushes grow thickly: almost
taking the place of grass near the hedge, for the water
of the brook moistens the ground. Sometimes the nests
of wild carrot occupy the sward, so numerous are
they. Cuckoo-flowers are dotted here and there.
Farther in the field, as it begins to rise, pale green cups
of cowslips hang, from which the yellow flower will
presently appear. A little farther up the slope, meadow
orchis grows: but hidden, from a distance, by the grass.

Earlier in the same June we saw two boys gathering
flowers in these meadows for sale: we called to them,
and they brought a half-bushel basket full, perfectly
full, of meadow orchis. The battered old basket, brown,
and dropping to pieces, was full to the brim of purple:
the ragged boys held it, one each side; they put it on the

sward and thrust their arms up to the elbows in bloom. A trifle of silver gladdened their hearts and they carried us home what we had bought—honest boys, though tattered, for they could easily have kept the money without delivering the flowers. We had enough to fill a large salad bowl, not the outside merely, but the entire bowl: a bowl full of purple to gloat over. These meadows, and particularly the first one, were thick with these flowers: so thick that we named them Orchis Meads. They are, too, always covered with cowslips.

As for the buttercups that year, in June they were not to be surpassed for the glory of their gold. There is a meadow—the one the partridges haunt by the Ewell Road—which was then simply hidden with them. There was no break: from hedge to hedge, it was just one breadth of yellow. The golden surface glistened with golden sheen: the reflected sunlight wavered over it, as heated air wavers. They stood high and so close together that the petals seemed to touch: the grass was invisible—roofed with gold. As a flat stone skims the water, making ducks and drakes, so it looked as if a stone might skim and slide along this burnished level. When the cows came in, they waded in flower to the middle as they wade in a pond. So that if the sky cleared for an hour the sun shone down on the most brilliant acres ever seen.

As that was one of the wettest, so the present spring has been one of the driest; and hence the marsh between the lane and the brook is accessible, the sedges low, the sandflags also, and the sedge-birds visible. The buttercups will not be a fifth so fine; nor is the orchis so plentiful. Still, walking along the roads, you see fragments of it, now and then, dropped by the flower hunters. This shortness of the sedges allows the marsh marigolds to show the more, and though not so forcing for some the dry weather is more suitable for other flowers.

There are three kinds of horse-tails about here. That which stands along the marsh, and in many of the adjacent meads is tall but pale; another kind creeps over the arable fields (as by Tolworth Brickfield); a third is now recently up (May) and rises from dry sandy ground, a short-joined stem with a knob of brown flower at the top covered with farina. These often thrust themselves up where moles have been stirring, as by the roads across these Orchis Meads; many appear by the race-course at Sandown at the time of the May races. Pink ragged robins flower along the hedge by the marsh as early as anywhere.

Some beech trees have a number of little branches round the trunk close to the ground—as a rule the beechbole is clear of boughs, but there are exceptions— and the leaves upon these particular branches remain on all the winter through. Those on the more important boughs above fall at the usual season; but, beneath, the foliage stays to rustle in the winter gales. A beech with such twigs stands on the verge of the brook by the road bridge; brown leaves are on it in December, and there they stay till the fresh green opens from the claw-like sheaths. Under the shelter of these brown leaves there was a flag, quite under them—the tip of the flag almost touching them—and all the winter through, despite the terrible frosts for which it was remarkable, despite its exceeding heavy snows and the bitter winds afterwards, there the plant remained green and fresh and never

The Last of a London Trout

withered. This beech droops the green leaves almost into the water, and casts a shadow under which my favourite trout used to often lie; to the boughs the willow wren comes and sings a little tremulous and pleading song. Beneath, the bank is a foot high or so, a tiny sandy cliff clothed with moss above, underneath which once there were shrew mice diving and racing about. It is curious that I have only seen them there once. A yard or two farther down, and still under the shadow of the beech, is a sandbank which is usually just above water, formed of particles cast up by the scour of the current under the arches of the bridge, and on the soft sloping sand the marks of moorhens' feet are often visible in autumn. A moorhen often stays under the arch on the Ewell side: if you remain still, she will soon reveal her presence by the ripple which comes out and which is easily distinguished from that caused by the

wind. When the ripple begins, the moorhen is moving; stand back and she will come out to the opening of the arch to feed on and among the weeds entangled in a hurdle kept there. It is always thick with water crow-foot, long green stalks with fringe-like ends, which floats down the brook, sometimes in great quantities when the ponds above are raked out. There was a water-rat sat on the hurdle which stands in the stream, nibbling these weeds, in the very midst of the sharpest weather last winter, when the snow was on the ground and the mud beside the brook frozen hard. So that, though they make nests and lay up hoards for a winter sleep, they do not slumber the whole time but come forth occasionally.

It was a sunny day, but the sunlight fell on frozen ground and water black by contrast with snow—the very bills of the geese seemed a deeper red in the sharp cold.

One got together forty potatoes for his store the autumn previous in Copper's field. In summer, I have seen them floating down the brook here with a flag in the mouth, the white part, which they like to eat, hard in the teeth and the long lead trailing behind. Their[17] feet and tails, too, often leave trails on the soft sandy ooze under the beech. It is so oozy that if the level of the brook be lowered and the support of the water partly withdrawn the sandbank immediately begins to crack and slip. At this moment a dam has been made across the brook above the bridge, and the side-hatch drawn so that the stream all runs through the old moat by Tolworth Court, so that the sandbank is entirely dry.

There is an inch or two of water at the very bottom of the brook still, and in this muddy pool—stagnant, too, or nearly—the other day I saw my trout. His coppery back came up to the surface and his spots showed as well as if you had held him in your hand. He was nosing about to find the meaning of the sudden loss of water and stinting of the large room he loved to roam in. He heaved himself over a dried branch that lay at the bottom, and well he did it, and this exhibited all his beauty, naked to the air and sunshine. He went away into the muddy shallows and was lost to sight. I hope he found his way to the arch of the bridge before his return thither was cut off by the drying up of the water. Under the arch—as is always the case—there remained a deep pool (the scour scoops out the bottom): I do hope he got there. But it was open to anyone to capture him who liked to face three inches of water and the mud, and I have been much distressed about him. He has had many escapes.

For a long time I had him to myself to admire; but one day a fool began at last to fish from the parapet of the bridge. It is past comprehension, but this fisherman had but paste on and was trying for bait when along came two navvies (trust a navvy to know!) —I was sitting on the white rails and I saw these two navvies, quite naturally, go up to the fisherman and look over the parapet. Instantly, they swore: and I shuddered, for I knew they had seen my beauty. They pointed him out to the fisherman—*who had been fishing right over the trout* and never saw it—and gave him directions what to do. There was a stir then and I walked mournfully away, not to see the end. But they did not succeed: he was too cunning and had slipped away under the arch. . . .*

This withy-bed is very thick and in it the moorhen and coot and water-rat, and all the creatures that love the waterside, find shelter. In autumn it turns white, rustling more as it dies, and the leaves stiffen; then, in the distant country, the fox, choosing the driest place, curls himself round by day in it. Where it grows on

* P. 52 of manuscript missing.

banks which, though close to water, are raised above
its level, hares are fond of it for their forms. Tallest,
thickest, and most luxurious of the grasses, there is none
like it to hide in.

Here, the level is too low and too often flooded for
game to stay, even if it were not so near the road. The
trees frequently stand in water; their leaves droop into
it, in autumn, and, falling several layers thick, there they
stay and do not decay for months. Flattened by the
presence of the water, these leaves lie with their edges
overlapping, and dyed brown and red and pale yellow,
with the clear water over, shadows thrown athwart,
and dry white reed grass around. Ice   sometimes forms
above them, like the glass above a picture.

A horse-chestnut drops its fruit in the dusty road: an
alder holds out its nut-like catkins; those of the aspen
are soft and quickly trodden into the dust by passers-by;
those of the alder remain on and are hard and lasting.

Down the lane where the withy-bed ends there is
another horse-chestnut whose bugles partly overhang
the brook. This is one of the trees especially to be noted
in autumn for the beauty of its foliage: for it is not all
trees, but only a few that come to perfection in this way.
These horse-chestnut sprays are loth to fall: the winds
pass over and the frosts bite them, yet they linger.
Presently they become a bright orange hue: orange is
not the correct term—it is almost scarlet, with an
orange tone in the background; the largeness of the leaf
and the breadth of the spray causes the colour to be
visible at a distance. Still, there are some green leaves;
the bugles begin to show and the trunk appears; underneath, the dark water flows, with a level surface; across
it, green meadow grass overhangs. There is scarlet and

orange above, and scarlet and orange below, the still, yet flowing, stream righting the colours.

Up in an ash which stands beside the lane, a thrush sings—they sing again in September—and this ash is the particular haunt of a thrush.

The water which keeps the fallen leaves is too much for flowers: even for the lesser celandine, which so much enjoys coolness and moisture but cannot flourish in actual water. The celandine therefore comes up where there are slight ridges, or near the road where the ground rises. Some dog-violets grow there, too.

Up-stream, looking over the parapet of the bridge, there is a plant growing at the bottom, a foot deep beneath the surface. It has pale, greenish-yellow leaves set equally each side of a slender stalk tipped with the lesser leaf. The weeds, the water-comfort or ranunculus, look natural under water, but this plant is not like a weed—its style and manner of growth are like the plants of the hedge banks, where, indeed, it often appears, dusty and dry, and far above the reach of any stream. It looks as if some plant had been artificially removed from the mounds and set under water. Waving to and fro with the current, it catches the eye immediately; it is a noisome thing; it is the water-parsnip, and a deadly poison. The brook is too broad and strong for it; it cannot flourish here, except perhaps at the side of the bridge, where there is a shallow place; but it fills the ditches and lesser streamlets, often where there is scarce a dribble of water, with long, thick, green stalks, hollow, and smelling strongly of parsnip if handled. It has a yellow flower. The thick growth of stalk and leaves which thus choke the ditches do not resemble the original plant, as here seen under the water, but they are from the same root. They have but a slight hold of the earth and are easily pulled up; the first flood sweeps them away.

A wooden bridge crosses the moat at the farmhouse, and as house-martins are continually going under it and stopping there, clinging to the side of the planking, probably they are building there: about two feet above the surface of the water. A pair built under the bridge in the arch. They frequently sweep at full speed through the arches, suddenly appearing underneath you as you look down. Some dead, dry bushes stand in the mud of the moat—in early spring when the sedge-birds first come to the withy-bed adjacent, they occasionally come across and perch on these twigs, where they can be better seen. But as the time advances and they become busy, courting and nesting, they do not roam so far. Sedge-birds or brook-sparrows are indeed the most stationary of birds; and, having once arrived and chosen their home, there they remain. They are constantly in motion, up this willow wand and then into this thicket of sedge, to and fro the willow stoles, but seldom wander outside their demesne of twenty yards circumference.

In that terrible year of rain, 1879, the hay crop in the meadow opposite, beside the brook, was carried away, floated across the road and under the arches, and lodged in a fringe of brown hay all round the verge of the farm garden within the moat. There it hung to the bushes, visible evidence of the loss farmers had to endure.

Purple loosestrife grows in one place on the shore of the moat, in summer, and also by the brook. This tall plant, like the iris, is absent from the banks of many brooks in the country: so is the yellow loosestrife so common by the Thames.

The pool under the arch left after the stream was turned by a dam through the side-hatch soon became clear, as the mud settled. It shrank a little, but not much; some showers fell and restored the evaporation. Day by day my dread increased, for the intelligence would get about that the brook was bayed, and the pools in its bed would be sure to attract attention. At last, on Sunday morning, the 22nd of May, what I had so long feared came about. Four men had attacked the last resort of my favourite trout. Two looked on and "helped", two waded in—one at each end of the arch— and stuck in the mud was a fish spear. As I came by, one man was already in at his mouth of the arch: the other sat on the grass taking off his stockings and rolling up his trousers, showing a powerful knee to the sunshine— a really fine knee which I could not help admiring. The next minute he was in the water, and the mud churned up by his feet began to darken and thicken it. He groped his way under the arch, and I hastened away— anxious not to see what I could not stop. Even though so hurt for my trout, could I honestly blame them? It was sport to them, and every man likes sport, and, were it in my power to give, should have it.

Yet my poor trout: he *could* not escape—there could be no loophole for him, could there, thus, in a narrow pool, bricked at the sides, a man at each end, the fish-spear ready hard by—no possible hope for him? I have been trying to think: was there a loophole? There could not be.

Chapter 3

TREES IN AND AROUND LONDON

STONY London is well wooded. The streets indeed are not planted with trees as they might have been had they been planned out instead of built haphazard. But there are parks and gardens in every direction just outside, and at the present day, at all events, wherever a tree can be put it is planted. So that despite certain notorious follies in dealing with the existing trees, even London itself the centre is on the whole well wooded. There is, of course, a difference of feeling, but generally I should not care to see trees in Cheapside, bustling crammed places are better without them: trees are not in accord with the spirit of the locality.

They want a quiet nook, or a broad open space, and there are plenty of these still treeless.

The Embankment, for instance, is most properly planted, so wide and sweeping a drive is the very spot, and there too they are seen to the best advantage. But, if I may venture an opinion, the wrong tree was chosen. Planes are not the best nor the finest trees. In the first place, they are not English. There are no planes in our hedgerows or coppices. They are not associated with green meadows, with yellowing wheat, with ancient mansions seen through branches, with gabled farmhouses and thatched cottages. There is no legendary event in English history connected with the plane, as there is with the oak, for instance. The plane is a foreigner and an interloper. It is not a stately tree: there are exceptions, of course; there is a really fine plane at

Kew, but, as a rule, the planes, which are common enough in the suburban gardens, are the very reverse of stately. A struggling, uncertain tree, it has no character.

Now the oak, the elm, the ash, these and many others have characters, and many of them form pictures in themselves, alone without accessories. He would be a bold artist who would paint a plane. It is true there is more than one kind of plane, but the Americans—good judges of timber, none better—look upon the plane with contempt, the despicable butter-nut tree, without use or ornament.

Our London planes have neither a lovely flower, edible fruit, or beautiful foliage. The trunks are always peeling: the outer bark comes off, leaving what would be white patches if it were not for the sooty particles which lodge upon them. These patches of dirty white look as if the tree suffered from some disease: a leprosy.

It has been said that the plane comes out into foliage before other trees, and continues later, affording the advantage of leaves for a longer period. I do not know of what particular species this is stated: but so far as regards the ordinary London plane, I emphatically deny it. Instead of coming into leaf before other trees, it is decidedly later; instead of retaining its leaves longer, it decidedly begins to drop them as soon as any, if not sooner than any. Hardly is the summer at its height before plane leaves begin to dot the ground like pieces of brown paper. The decaying leaf of the plane lacks everything that makes the dying leaf of other trees so beautiful. It is brown paper simply; brown blotches on the lawn. It no sooner begins to turn colour than down it comes.

There is a suburban garden of which I have taken

particular notice, because two or three large planes stand in it with a beech between them. The difference is indeed astonishing. The planes turn brown and at once the lawn is covered with these blotches. The beech first shows golden spots among its green branches: no one surely could pass without admiring it. After a while the yellow spreads. By and by every leaf takes a tint which, for want of better terms, may be called orange red. Still lingering on the boughs, the leaves gradually become redder and browner, and then at last fall. The contrast could scarcely be greater. The beech is a picture in itself: when the sunshine falls on it, it is lit up with glowing tints.

In the spring, again, the gradual progress of the buds of the beech afford a daily pleasure: the sheaths opening and the leaves coming forth.

If the plane can show anything as interesting, it lifts its branches so far above that it cannot be watched.

The only time the plane looks well is just after it has arrived at full leaf: then, of course, it is green and pleasant, but it shares this with every tree; it would not be a tree at all if it did not, and it is soon over; in a brief while its green becomes dusty and dull.

Birds do not like the plane: they do not recognize it; they would rather go to any other tree; they may use it if they can get no other and have no choice. You can see at a glance that it is not well suited for nest building.

The elm, long before it spreads the leaf, fills the mind with hope of spring, with the reddish hue in its upper branches.

The oak not only has its own autumn colours, but it has a spring colour and is a ruddy copper before it is green.

The horse-chestnut delights everyone with its blossom; its fruit, if not edible, has a fine colour.

The miserable plane alone stands bare and gaunt, a tree in name and nothing more. In its own country, with its natural surroundings, doubtless it is good to

look at. In our green island, it is not. No one who has ever lived among hedgerows can like it: it is the tree of the cabinet naturalist, of the nursery gardener. The only reflection in its favour on the Embankment is that we must be thankful to see trees at all. There might have been none: there is that to be said. It is asserted indeed that the plane resists the gases in the atmosphere better than other trees. So far at least as the Embankment is concerned, this argument is out of court. There is a constant current of air along the river; you can always get a breeze there; indeed, if anyone is jaded or fatigued, they cannot do better than turn aside from the roar of the Strand and in three minutes find themselves inhaling fresh air.

The argument is equally out of place in large open spaces like Hyde Park. Is it really founded upon fact at all? Are there not elms in the heart of the city, flourishing vigorously? I know plenty in dingy places enough in all conscience. Those that perish, as I have shown elsewhere,* do so from underground injury: from new sewers carrying away water, from gas-impregnated soil, and injury to roots. From these causes they die on the summit of elevations ten miles from Charing Cross, exposed to all the winds of heaven.

Imagine the Embankment, the finest site in Europe, with a double avenue of elms: there might have been a rookery; rooks have no objection to houses. Or with beeches, all aglow in autumn.

[Oaks are slow, it is true, but beautiful. Horse-chestnuts grow quickly—as quickly as planes—and they would have lined the river wall with snowy bloom. But we have, instead, miserable planes; and are thankful, as we might have had nothing.]

As hedges turn into country villages and there are corners of fields and little plantations among the houses, so garden lands run into London. Some of the suburbs are almost lost in orchards, and orchard gardens; others are full of trees. In one or two places the trees indeed are so numerous that they are rather encumbrances. So much moisture is not altogether desirable; the air is prevented from circulating and the earth never properly dries; nor can the light, that greatest of all sanitary agents, purify the surface with its subtle influence.

Judicious thinning out is required, but that is quite a different thing from destruction. When people of necessity live close together, it is questionable whether the too near proximity of trees is healthy. A house in the middle of a field is one thing: you may plant trees all round till the boughs touch the windows. But semi-detached villas, or detached (i.e., eight feet between), row after row, block after block, are another thing. Trees

* *Nature Near London.*

crowded around such buildings keep off both air and light, and air and light are life itself. Plant them at the end of the lawn or in the street: then they will do good.

One most injurious thing in the suburbs is the high brick garden walls, and equally high palings. Every little villa has its garden of fifty feet square surrounded with walls high enough to close in a nunnery. These are most unhealthy. In some suburbs, even on considerable hills, they quite prevent the circulation of air. You may walk over such villa-studded hills with a high wind blowing and scarce feel a puff. If the streets were all in one parallel line, the breeze would enter and rush through, but the roadways of London suburbs are very involved and the most uproarious gale cannot blow round a hundred corners. The atmosphere therefore quite stagnates. Up above, in the tops of the elms, there is a sweet breeze; below, in the carefully laid out gardens, for which large rents are paid, there is not a breath. In summer, consequently, the heat is intense: in autumn, the odour of decaying leaves is never blown away: in winter, the soil never dries—the frost either is or seems to be more severe because the earth is damp. These solid garden walls are, therefore, distinctly antagonistic to health [and, attached as I am to trees, I cannot but think that it is possible to have too many in thickly populated districts.]

The sensation in walking through such suburbs on a warm summer day is as if you wanted to breathe but could not. The Embankment, though it passes through the centre of London, is preferable.

Passing on again, one step farther from the City, and coming to the large villas—mansions they would be called in the country—which really stand in their own grounds, and which are so numerous all around the verge of the suburbs, one thing occurs to me most forcibly. It is the absence, shall we say the banishment, of English trees and shrubs. If English trees, elm or oak, chance to be there, growing, when the villa is built, of course, they are left; but no others are planted. Do you ever see young oaks in these grounds, some of which are really small parks? Do you ever see young elms? I do not think I ever saw a young ash: the ash is even more rare than the others. Planes are planted (miserable planes), cedar Deodara, various other cedars, thick shrubberies of laurel, thickets of rhododendrons, sumach, and endless other foreign trees and shrubs. The very titles of the curious trees planted in such places would fill a book: they are drawn from all the countries of the earth—from all, rather, except England. The one primary rule appears to be: Let there be nothing English!

It is possible to understand the natural desire to possess a rare tree or shrub when it first arrives in this country; experiments in growing the blue gum, or the bamboo, or papyrus, have a distinct interest in themselves. But it is difficult indeed to understand the singular frame of mind which stocks its grounds from the nursery garden, with the same laurels, cedars, sumachs, the very identical shrubs to be seen in every neighbour's enclosure.

One might walk in many London suburbs for miles through roads lined on either hand with villas whose occupants must, from the very fact of their being able to pay such rents, receive large incomes. Yet the shrubs, trees, and plants in their gardens are all exactly alike. The effect is wearisome in the extreme, far more so than the garden-less houses of London streets. When, however, one sees the same thing repeated in the small parks just alluded to, the marvel is still greater. It is not for want of money: that is certain; for the sums expended on such grounds would keep a small country house, and maintain a conveyance.

Why nothing but evergreen foreign shrubs? Why nothing English? Of all the foreign shrubs that have ever been brought to these shores, there is not one that presents us with so beautiful a spectacle as the bloom of the common, old English hawthorn in May. The mass of blossom, the delicacy of each particular spray of flower, the tint of each particular petal, the pleasant fragrance, and then the old traditions and associations of the May, place it far, far above the finest of the exotic importations.

Then, again, the old hedge crab—the common, despised crab—in spring is covered with rosy pink, all bloom: you may distinguish it in the hedgerow, or on the hillside, half a mile away. Compare the crab with a plane or a laurel, and where are the latter? They have not a chance in the competition.

There is, too, the interest in our own old English trees and shrubs which arises from watching their progress with the season: their buds literally keep pace with the stars, the buds on the common crab thickening at the tip and opening as Sirius sinks to the West and Arcturus advances towards the zenith. There is a correspondence between the hedge and the heavens: the whole face of nature changes in harmony.

How pleasant it is to see the clear white flower of the blackthorn come out in the midst of the bitter easterly breezes: it is like a flag of truce hung out to winter on the hedge. There will not be much more frost; if the wind is bitter to-day, the sun is rapidly gaining. I presume if a blackthorn bush were by any chance discovered in the small parks which I have alluded to, it would at once be rooted out as an accursed thing.

The very bramble bushes of our hedges are beautiful, and well worthy to be encouraged to grow in the finest park ever yet enclosed. What, pray, is a pitiful laurel beside a bramble bush? Not only the bramble flower, the berry is delicious. I mean to say that the flavour of the common blackberry is delicious, and would be thought an extreme delicacy did it come from abroad.

As for the roses, the dear old roses, the June rose, and the trailing rose, I defy the world to produce anything equal to them. But these are briars and thorns—root them up! They are English—let us have miserable planes and pitiful laurels!

In the foreign evergreen, the autumn colours—one half the charm of the year—are absent. The common dogwood, for instance, has not only a white flower but, so soon as touched by the frosts, the leaves turn red and bronze. The wild guelder rose, too, is superior to the garden species, for it produces heavy bunches of red berries. Then there is the way-faring tree, and let us have clematis—wild "honesty"—everywhere we can. And the hazel—fill the nooks and corners with nut-tree stoles, instead of spindly laurels again, poked in and looking like the wooden shrubs of children's toys.

This is the merest, most superficial, sketch of what might so easily be effected in this way. Besides our trees and shrubs, there are our wild flowers, whose name is legion, but which are carefully eradicated from these grounds.

The Old House at Coate

Enter a copse in spring and the eye will be delighted with cowslips in the banks where the sunlight comes; with bluebells among the stoles; with anemones in the shade; with rising ferns: but enter the "pleasure" grounds of a modern villa-mansion and they are bare. In the waters to be found in such places it is a hundred to one if you see a reed, a yellow iris or a bulrush.

Besides what I contend is the greater beauty of our own old English trees, shrubs, and plants, these also attract all kinds of birds and animals. Hawthorn is the favourite bush with every wild creature in this country. Plant hawthorn and you are certain to have birds.

For myself, I would prefer thistles to planes and laurels. The thistles would please me with mauve and purple flowers; the humble-bees would come to them, and, later on, the goldfinches.

While proceeding outwards, you step farther: from the Embankment to the suburbs; from the villas to the small parks; and now to the first glimpses of the open country. I may repeat the words with which I began: that London is well wooded. It is well surrounded, too, with open spaces, commons, or let us call them rather wildernesses, since some commons are quite bare; but these I mean are full of vegetation. There are fern-grown dells on Wimbledon Common—one close to the spot where the shooting takes place at the Running Deer—equal to any in the most distant country. It is difficult to believe, indeed, when standing on the high ground there, looking over the wooded country before one, that London is so near; and that the omnibus, that distinctive London vehicle, starts from an inn close at hand. From the high ground by the Crystal Palace, again, there are trees, trees, trees, in every direction.

Beckenham is rapidly falling, it is true, before the inevitable bricks and mortar; but still the environs are full of trees. Hayes Common there in early summer is a lovely spot; when I saw it, it was one broad mass of gold, every furze bush aglow with bloom, bees humming, butterflies floating, swallows whirling, the air dim with the peculiar luxurious haze of sunshine. Yet, yonder, could be seen the tall   factory chimneys, I suppose of Bermondsey or Deptford, toned down by the vaporous atmosphere to slender minarets. From Epsom Downs, if you will walk aside a few minutes from the Derby crush, the view is most pleasing. Hills, vales, plains, and all wooded. You may easily tell, when looking over a Surrey landscape, where modern life is clustering, by the white steeples. The old Surrey churches seem rarely to have had spires, or spires of the lowliest description. Look, for instance, at Chessington (if you can find it), or Thames Ditton church, where the borage sheds its blue petals so thickly on the tombs. Where white steeples stand up sharp and clear, there modern villas will be found in abundance. At Epsom, in passing, the weed fumitory, so often mentioned in old books, grows in the arable fields: I only note it because in so many places high husbandry has quite banished it.

The   name Chessington may easily be discovered on the map, but the place is another matter. There are meadows and woods; there is a church, a farm-house, three cottages. It is as isolated, as thoroughly a hamlet, as the smallest in the distant western counties. When I strayed there by chance, the clergyman, or curate, happened to come along the footpath; he eyed me as the natives of America eyed Columbus!

And so you may stray in Surrey: southwards and westwards, always among trees and woods, and copses, and endless commons, ever going deeper and deeper into true country, with every species of bird and animal life around you, and something to explore ahead, and yet the beginning of your trail shall start from a station within twenty-five or thirty minutes of Westminster.

I have said nothing of the north because it is not well known to me, but others report it as equally wooded.

So that London is now as it was in the days of Cæsar, a town in the midst of woods.

Mistletoe grows in Bushey Park, close to Hampton Court, on the hawthorn bushes to the left of the first fountain. Last Mayday there were still berries adhering to two pieces of mistletoe; some of the berries were very large. Jackdaws are so numerous there, and in Hampton Court Park, that they almost equal the rooks. The flocks are often composed nearly equally of rooks and jackdaws: in country places the rooks usually much outnumber the latter. Half a dozen jackdaws seem there to enliven a whole army of rooks, while here the rooks are occasionally at least in the minority.

Just above Molesey Lock, in the meadows beside the towing path, the blue meadow geranium or crane's bill grows in large bunches among the mowing grass in summer. It is one of the most beautiful flowers of the field: after having lost sight of it for some years, to see it again at last seemed indeed to bring the old familiar country near London.

Between Hampton Court and Kingston, the towing path is bordered by a broad green sward sufficiently extensive to be worth mowing. In July last I observed a man at work here in advance of the mowers pulling

up the yarrow with might and main: the herb grew
in such quantities that it was necessary to remove it first,
or the hay would be too coarse. He said that persons
came for it sometimes and took away a whole trap
load: the flowers were to be boiled and mixed with

cayenne pepper for cold in the chest. In spring, the
dandelions here are pulled in sackfuls to be eaten as
a salad. This sort of thing has so much fallen into
disuse in the country that it was a surprise to me to
find the herbalist in a measure flourishing round about
London.

By Teddington Lock I once noticed broom rape
growing on the bank: this curious plant looks as if it
had been buried in earth—earthed-up as gardeners do
certain salads—and had thereby been prevented from
becoming green.

Lurchers are not uncommon round London: I often
see them; poaching goes on, to some small extent, in the
fields which are not preserved but border on the preserves; and once I saw a very bold attempt from a trap
with a fast horse in the shafts.

Summer, I am sure, arrives sooner near London, and
lingers later: it is already spring in southern London
while it is yet winter but a few miles distant.

The Old House at Coate

The blue veronica fills the grass with beauty: the tree-pipits sing, sing on the oaks and descending to the ground; by and by, the silky barley waves softly to the breeze.

There are so many pleasant villages round about: there is a spot at Ewell where an old mill-wheel goes rumbling round and round, with a clear millpool, a bent fir leaning over the water, an old punt half sunk, moorhens and dab-chicks swimming and diving, which, if it were painted, would be believed to exist in some far-away country. At night, the light of the lantern gleams across the pool; a star shines in the dark water, deep down—still and bright, while the rumbling wheel goes round, grinding our bread.

But where shall I cease? These miscellaneous notes I have thrown together just to show that one could go wandering round the rim of the mighty city, ever coming upon something new and yet old.

There are odd names of places in distant counties—none odder than Half Smock, which appears in the Surrey map.

Even hard, prosaic Clapham Junction is not quite without animal life. Eleven hundred trains go booming, shrieking, rattling through that place every day. Yet at night, while waiting in one of the rooms (bare enough they are) of the middle platforms, after alighting to change from the Brighton train, I have seen the timid mice come out, like swift animated shadows, and move across under the table, searching no doubt for the crumbs left by passengers. One would have imagined that eleven hundred trains would scare every creature to a distance.

From the dry gravel paths—hard, suburban paths,

the roadway one side, garden walls the other—the winged ants rise in summer; and thus nature is everywhere.

And nature knows no books: children in their wild joy with a cowslip come nearest to her. I dislike the term "natural history": lists, and classifications, and Latin names, have no meaning to me. They have their uses, but quite beside my purpose.

There is more botany in one garden buttercup than in all the shrivelled herbariums of the whole world.

Hard and stony as London is, there are meadows round about it, any one of which could offer a buttercup to every single person in it, and still have plenty.

THE ENGLISH BREED

Chapter 1

THREE CENTURIES AT HOME*

THE thought occurred to me: suppose the written
records of English history were swept away and
an inquiring spirit like Herodotus went about collecting
from popular tradition and national monuments the
story of the past, what a strange and interesting work
it would be! Imagine Clarendon and Macaulay, Bacon
and other great authors, quite extinct, or retained only
in unreadable hieroglyphics, and our Herodotus gravely
stepping into Westminster Abbey, listening, half
credulous, half critically, to the attendants' tales of the
Richards, and Edwards, and Henrys, and calmly jotting
them down in his note-book!

See him walking over Bosworth field; or at Battle,
visiting the site of the Saxon's woe; or on the ridge of
White Horse Hill, harkening to the shepherd's legend
of Alfred the Great, and his horn of stone. Imagine a
history of England compiled in the same way as these
local records, for they are all from life.

It was something in this way that history was first
written; and it is not difficult to believe that our own
would be as full of demi-gods and heroes and marvellous
exploits as that of the Trojan war, were the same
method pursued at this day.

The past fades so very quickly. The class of cattle and
sheep of a few centuries ago have passed away, have
changed altogether, so have the men and even the dogs.

* M.S. dated 1877.

The Old House at Coate

From oral inquiry what could not we have gleaned of times as near our own as the Corn Law sufferings and the times of Riot and the Enclosures of the Common Lands.

In endeavouring to write about the past, we must dimly photograph the present.

How was history first written? What part did the collection of oral tradition from the lips of illiterate people play in its shaping? I would have my material gathered in large part from illiterate persons, and thus I would write my new Saxon Chronicle.

Full of this idea, I set out in my own village to learn from the unlettered our local history, and what in their living belief were the deeds of the men of yore.

As the operations of the human mind, especially among the illiterate, are supposed to be almost identical, it is possible that the result may present some analogies casting light upon the growth of ancient fable.

(Though real names of persons and places are, for obvious reasons, varied, these home-annals are literally rendered from life.)

(But the inquiry need not be confined to one village, half a dozen would do. A territory, say, the course of the edge of a hill, Wolston to Avebury.)

Mr. Jonathan Browne was leaning against a stile watching his lambs at play when I asked him, as the first person I met, what he could tell me of the past. He is one of Mr. Carlyle's "grey-men". Years of hard life, and storm and labour, have silvered his brown hair, and thinned it over his temples, but his form is upright, his blue eyes brilliant and piercing—there is intense, *stern* energy in his very voice—something in the whole man that recalls the ideal of the sea-king's followers of old.

He is not contemplating those skipping lambs with a view to pastoral poetry. His poetry is not of words and phrases—his life is a rude stanza, hammered out by knocks, and blows, of wind and hail and snow and summer's heat; such a stanza as could not be penned

with quill and ink, but must be graven with steel tool upon stone. It will be cut some day in the old church-yard, one more line added to the slow growing poem of ten generations. So long at least has his family dwelt on their narrow acres of freehold. There he stands now, grey, stern, upright, like a landmark himself. A great noble head: a head somewhat resembling that of Vespasian on antique coins; but silent. He has seen much, thought much, done much, in that little country, his own parish: but spoken nothing. Is it not better, grander, so? We are so overwhelmed with words now. It is doubtful if he has ever written anything beyond his own name—painted, rather than written, labori-ously up and down, with stiff fingers and heavy hand.

"My grandfather," said he, "used to say he knew a man when he was young who had fought in his youth against Prince Charlie at Culloden."

"What was your grandfather's age and when did he die?"

The Old House at Coate

"He died in 1868, aged eighty-four."

"This is 1877, and Culloden was fought in 1745, i.e., just thirty-nine years before he was born. Supposing the soldier to have been twenty at the time of the battle, he would be fifty-nine at your grandfather's birth. But your grandfather would hardly remember such a conversation before he was fifteen—the soldier would then be seventy-four."

Like this, I thought, the writers of the Anglo-Saxon Chronicle must have got at their facts. When they attempted to put down records they inquired of the warriors who had fought. They must have compiled their information from the tradition of old men. What did the soldier tell him about the battle? But here came a blank. The soldier died and was buried in the parish churchyard, and that was all: except that "Charlie" was beaten. So that writing history in this way would almost exactly reproduce the Saxon chronicle: "This year Cedric fought against the Britons, and overcame them."

"The thing is quite possible, evidently. So that yours, your grandfather's, and the soldier's memories—three only—go back one hundred and thirty-two years: an average of forty-four years each. This is bridging time."

Of the Civil War, of William III, of Waterloo even, he had no tradition. They had passed away utterly except as names. But I could read all about them in books. That was not it. Well, perhaps old Willis, the shepherd, could tell me something.

Willis came, bent double, or nearly, yet with a cheerful face, if that which was so battered by tempest and rain could be called a face. He had grown insensible to the weather; he had no ambitions or hopes beyond a pint of beer; and, instead of melancholy, he seemed to have reached a species of Nirvana at three score and eight. He had a coin he had picked up in the turnip field, hoeing, after rain; on examination, it proved to be a sixpence of Charles II, much worn.

"What did you do with the cannon ball you found in the Chace, John?" said Mr. Browne.

The boys had had it to play with and it was lost. It was about the size of an apple—a fair-sized codling, and terribly rusty. It was one that Oliver Cromwell had shot off, no doubt.

[He had heard that once upon a time some titled traitor withdrew the flints from the muskets of a body of English troops, substituting wooden ones, which, of course, could not ignite the powder and they were defeated. Of date, place, and person he had no knowledge.]

Cromwell and Julius Cæsar are the two names around which every local tradition of fighting gathers. The ancient earthworks and Roman coins are always relics of the divine Julius. If some once painted windows in the Church are now plain, it was Cromwell's fist that smashed them. My Clarendon, however, says that there actually was a skirmish near this Chace—now but a few disconnected beech coppices—though before Oliver had risen to command. Oliver, like Virgil in Italy, is at the bottom of all mischief.

The shepherd could not even recollect anything of George III—the mark left by the Georges was but an evanescent one—except the great copper pennies. These he deeply regretted. You could buy three times as much with one of these: once he found a packet, five shillingsworth of them, wrapped in paper, in a rabbit-hole near the highway, when cutting a hedge. Probably some thief had hidden them. There were more half pence used then than now. The shepherd did not see that the relative value of the metals had changed since his youth: his faith was firm in copper. Once his cousin Thomas helped to dig the coach of the great Duke of Wellington out of a drift of snow in which it was half buried. They took hurdles from the fields and laid them on the snow to form a firm ground for the wheels. That was all he knew about Waterloo. He had confused memories of the machine riots, of the use by the peasantry of prongs and flails in an insurrection, of the burning of ricks and the use of the yeomanry. His own father, he said, was pricked with a sword as he scrambled through a hedge.

"Old Betsy would tell you more, perhaps," said Mr. Browne. "They say she's a hundred years old." He took me to her cottage, which had once been a small farm-house on a dairy farm. In some countries it is common to find this, as the little holdings are bought up and added to the larger properties.

The cottage door was open in the warm summer afternoon, and the bees were busy in the honeysuckle of the wooden porch. A besom was leant against the wall —not required at that season: but in winter to be used by visitors to brush the mud from their boots after crossing the meadows. "Come in," said a thin, toothless voice in answer to a tap, and entering, I saw the old lady sitting at her spinning-wheel.

The old lady sat before the fire—a few wood embers —with the spinning-wheel beside her. This was indeed going back into the past. I had thought that the spinning-wheel was quite extinct: only known by pictures of ancient interiors of the Dutch school, or perhaps seen for a brief space upon the stage in the chamber of love-stricken Margaret. Here it was really in use. She was making mops out of wool which she collected at the spring sheep-washings. From medieval times at these sheep-washings, the labourers at the dipping stick to their rights. She nodded to Mr. Browne familiarly: but rose and curtseyed to me, as a stranger, and with trembling hands and knotted fingers pulled forward a chair for me, telling me to keep my hat on, which I had of course removed. Old country folks think it no discourtesy to retain their hats on a visit.

She could not tell me the year in which she was born; she calculated her age by the thatch. The house had been new thatched four times since she could remember. She was a great girl when it was done the first time, because father fell from the ladder and broke his arm—that she recollected well. Father thatched it twice. Her own husband thatched it the third time, and the fourth was three years ago. I could see it if I liked—"it were amazing thick."

Mr. Browne and I measured it roughly; we found it between eight and nine feet in thickness. The farmer said a good coat of straw would last twenty years: four coats represented eighty years; add three years since the last thatching, and say the old lady was seven when her father broke his arm, and that would make her ninety.

The thread she was spinning was very coarse and was for mops. These she made herself, and then trudged round the parish to sell them at the farm-houses. The wool was obtained from the sheep-dipping pools: being caught in a fishing-net. When the sheep were dipped they struggled a good deal, and pieces of wool came out:

these floated down the stream and were intercepted by the net stretched across. The washing of some thousands of sheep yielded a very considerable quantity of wool in this way, to which was added the pieces she could pick up in the fields, torn out by bushes and brambles, and even adhering to stout thistles. The shepherds insist upon their absolute legal rights to the use of these dipping pools, based upon immemorial custom. To hear them talk about it has often reminded me of the disputes concerning wells in the days of the patriarchs: and indeed these pools are almost as important to the flock owners as the wells and springs of the deserts were to the flocks of Job.

Mr. Browne said there was one other old woman in the parish who still used the spinning-wheel; there had been three, but the third died a short time since. She knew nothing whatever of history beyond remembering the ringing of the church bells for the victory of Nelson. But she could, she said, sing me "The Leathern Bottle", or tell me a tale. Preferring the tale, she began the history of a stupid fellow upon whose head his mother rained down raisins from a first floor window, in order to conceal an amour, in which, though somewhat distorted, I readily recognized one of the stories of the *Pentamerone* of the Queen of Navarre. As she could not read or write, the difficulty was to account for the transmission of the story from so distant a source into a little benighted western hamlet. All she knew was that she had heard it from her mother. It would be interesting to ascertain at what date the first English translation of the *Pentamerone* was published. Students of mythology are well aware of the curious appearance of legends among nations apparently quite disconnected.

Three Centuries at Home

I was told of a drinking farmer, who used to fill the kettle with gin instead of hot water.

Incidentally, talking of her only son, who was dead, the strong belief the peasantry still retain in the efficacy of herbs exhibited itself. He slowly wasted away with an abscess, despite the best medical advice obtained through the kindness of the vicar. But, if she could only have walked up into Berkshire, and seen a little old man at a certain village there, near the river Kennet, he would have given her a water-herb which was an absolute specific for abscess. She regretted her inability to walk the distance to that day, and no one would go for her. So her son died, all for the want of a simple herb growing by the river.

OHC-I

Chapter 2

STRENGTH OF THE ENGLISH*

I

NATURE has designed the English race for strength. This appears upon comparing the form of a fairly built Englishman with the models left by the ancients in the Hercules and Antinous. The Antinous it is true is the ideal of graceful manhood, but it is a manhood which with labour would obviously develop into the possession of great vigour. In the Hercules the muscles are carried to a round fullness, which while indicating enormous power still leaves an impression of just proportion. A fairly built Englishman can hold his own in the comparison with these ancient models of strength and latent power. Our hands alone prove it. They are broad, brown, and hard: specially fitted for the spade, the axe and the sword. The thumb is large, its base[1] firm; the joints big, and the nail wide and thick. The knuckles stand out, when the hand is clenched, like knots; the fingers are broad and squarish, and the tips somewhat blunt. To the touch, the palm is firm; the back of the hand is rather rough, and it is thick through. At the wrist, the bones are prominent: so too the sinews; the wrist, indeed, is like a pole in those who have been used to labour. The entire hand speaks of physical force. It can dig, and dig deep and continuously: it can chop, day after day, till the forest is thinned; it can haul the tarred ropes and hoist the sail, or heave up the anchor

* M.S. dated 1884.

at the capstan. Lastly, it can fight. A blow from it, delivered straight from the shoulder, would infallibly break the jaw, were it to be received full without check from an intervening arm. If it struck in the rear of the ear, death might follow. Ribs, arm bones, even breast bones, have been crushed in by this hand. In the heroic age, Ulysses broke his opponent's jaw with a single blow, and it is recorded as an instance of his strength. There are hundreds of men among us at the present day who could do the same thing with ease. No cunning of fence could defend the best swordsman against a real assault from such hands as these armed with rifle and bayonet. One swordsman may face and foil one man with the bayonet; but ten men with the bayonet must perforce overcome ten swords. In such hands as these, the bayonet, which is in fact a short spear, is irresistible. These broad, brown, hard hands, in close combat, must of necessity prevail—and they are always anxious for close combat. As they can dig, their utility in the trenches is evident; the idea of winning battles by the spade comes to them naturally, so that a general who has an army of such hands has a clear course before him. Set them to dig, and bring them to close hand-to-hand conflict.

"The weight of his fist" is a saying full of meaning. Such hands can go through the panel of a door, splintering the wood; they have been known to fell an ox. They are seen in rudest perfection among labourers who have worked in the field from boyhood: seamen and artisans accustomed to heavy tools. But the very largest and most powerful—exceptionally so—are found among farmers, who have not only laboured as hard or harder than their men in the open air but have enjoyed the advantage of better food. Here and there a hand may be observed among the farming class which is truly gigantic in its proportion. Such a hand ought to be sculptured: it is far more powerful than that with which Hercules is shown. It is less graceful in outline, but in the grace of sheer power—absolute strength—it is superior. These classes excel in this particular because the circumstances in which they are placed are favourable to such development. But the same tendency is equally present among the population of cities, as in London, and even among the upper, moneyed, or normally idle, section. The hands are whiter, the joints less pronounced, the skin softer, the wrist flatter, instead of almost round, and the nails narrower and thinner. But the tendency is there all the same. A little work, a little exercise, and the hereditary disposition will display itself. They will not, of course, at once become so large and strong. It may well be that the individual has not only not been accustomed to manual labour, but that his parents and grandparents were likewise able to live without it. These points have therefore been toned down, but if the circumstances were reversed they would soon appear again. It is surprising, too, what latent possibilities of strength exist in these white, slender, and apparently effeminate hands. After a few weeks' training the sinews obtain a wirelike toughness. The stamina is there, inherited through centuries: it only needs the opportunity to exhibit itself.

2

The arm of a man who has laboured from boyhood corresponds in size to his hand. We traced it to the wrist. Beyond that, the two bones of the lower arm are somewhat far apart, much farther than in the arm unused to work. The upper arm is largest at the shoulder and immediately beneath it. Now in the Hercules, the classic model of strength, all the muscles of the arm are equally developed and stand out in finely curved masses. This is not the case in the English arm. That part of it near the shoulder is more prominent in proportion than the rest. The muscle which forms a kind of ball or egg upon bending the elbow is not so decided as in the ancient statue. This is the muscle which lifts, or pulls. There is more mass, more development, at the back part of our arms. Those are the muscles which push, swim and strike. The egg or ball is seen well developed in persons who have specially devoted themselves to certain athletic sports. In some individuals it is present naturally. It was observable in the Zulu arms. I noticed it very strongly once in the arm of an Italian athlete who was displaying feats of strength with weights in the street. His form was well moulded and immediately recalled the antique cast of strength. Our arms easily acquire that peculiarity but I do not think it is so common among us as the development of the shoulder, the arm just below it, the muscles at the back, and the remarkable width of the lower arm. The three first are singularly prominent in the arm of Captain Webb, the arm that swam the Channel. His arm about the shoulder is of immense size. In labourers, artisans, farmers and others accustomed to manual labour of more varied kind, the space between the two bones already mentioned is most marked.

3

The back, the chest, and, generally, the torso, are disposed to squareness. There are many labourers, workmen and others, who exhibit great width of chest, but the measurement of the most powerful is as much made up by thickness as by breadth alone. Many are almost as thick as wide. And when they have reached their fullest development they have scarcely any waist, but are nearly the same size all down. Consequently, there is an absence of "figure": there is no elegance, but there is wonderful immobility—the immobility of the oak trunk. This is a kind of make which is very difficult to throw in wrestling: the man stands as if rooted to the ground. I think that the very finest men in sheer power of torso are found among seamen. I do not mean the brave fellows penned in ironclads, nor those who work steamers. I mean the genuine seaman who can reef a sail in a barge and hang on by his eyelashes. Perhaps the fishermen (not the long-shore fellows) who go out in the cutters answer to the description best nowadays. The extraordinary development of the back, the chest, and the body generally, attained by these men must be almost unsurpassed. Why do not the sculptors study them? Why do they for ever repeat the same models? Why not give us an English Hercules?

This size, squareness, and thickness of body is as characteristic as the shape of the hand. Perhaps it is the enormous breadth, thickness, and firmness of the torso which especially distinguishes us. The ancient model is as flexible as strong. We have not the pliability of form,

nor the exact proportion. We have on the other hand
a larger share of solid, immovable strength. The lower
limbs answer to the torso: they are brawny and sturdy,
rather than graceful, in the ordinary sense of the word;
but strength has a grace of its own. There is nothing

ideal or exceptional in this description. It has been
derived from broad and general observation, and not
from any selected models. All men, indeed, are not
alike: but the race has a universal tendency to the
physical development which has been depicted.

The life of cities is unfavourable to it, no doubt. The
stooping over desks and counters, the indoor confinement, the sedentary engagements, even the food (much
of it over-stimulating), and the nervous anxieties inseparable from "business", are detrimental. But so in-
eradicable is the inherited tendency that even these,

though sustained for several generations, fail to over-come it.

4

In London, the city with which I am best acquainted, I frequently meet men of fine and stalwart proportions. I constantly meet men fully up to or above the average size, and once now and then persons who far exceed it. Stand back a little, for instance, from the traffic in the Strand, Fleet Street, Cheapside, or any central and important thoroughfare, and watch the human stream. Hundreds upon hundreds—say, rather, thousands upon thousands—of persons pass whose stature and size is rather above the average. In the crowd, men frequently go by who excel in these respects, and occasionally one who towers above the level like a giant. How often, too, while standing in a crowded assembly you find your-self quite overtopped and looked down upon by such an individual! I am at present referring to well-dressed people, and I venture to say that if a measurement were made of every such person who walked down either of the above streets during an hour there would be found far more above the average than under it. A little man would be rarer than a giant. A very good spot to see this is on London Bridge from four to seven of an afternoon when the people are rushing off to the terminus. There is a never-ending crowd of tall fellows of their inches.

So far from degeneration are the well-to-do Lon-doners that I deliberately affirm them to be a large-made people. When a person has been accustomed to indoor life from childhood, has never known manual labour, or exposure to the weather, of course his sinews cannot be so strong; nor can he present so hardy an appearance as would be the case under opposite circumstances. But the size is there; the potential strength is there, and the potential power of endurance. In short, there is splendid material.

This fact may very well escape the notice of those whose whole time has been spent in the midst of it. Business men hasten along—time is money—and take no account of the masses about them. The trees are so thick you cannot see the wood. But let anyone go away from it for a while upon the Continent, and then upon returning bear the point in mind. It will be at once evident. As for the workmen, no words are needed. Some trades must, of course, be admitted as exceptions: trades which entail much confinement. But wherever manual labour is required, and muscular energy is called into play, the London workman is as burly, as large, and as powerful, as any.

Descending to the lowest class of all, what bone and size do we not often see in the idlers and the beggars? In short, this country teems with strong men.

A very large number, too, of those who are some-times contemptuously called "weeds" are unjustly despised. After a time and under different circumstances many of them become well proportioned. Youths frequently grow too fast, particularly when they are not checked by manual labour, but are stimulated by rich food. The sons of wealthy parents, in cities, often seem at first, as it were, to run to seed, and exhibit undue length of limbs and narrowness of chest. Others, again, seem all out of shape and loose-jointed; and others are found to be painfully weak when unexpectedly called upon to endure fatigue. From these appearances all sorts of evils are predicted, and it is confidently asserted that the unfortunate lad will never come to anything. Nothing can be less true. The feeblest children often grow into the strongest men. The despised "weed" in the course of a few years becomes healthy, widens out, and walks upright as a bolt. Care should be taken that the "weed" be not over-exercised while in the condition of "weediness". Too much athleticism at that date may strain him and leave him in a permanent state of feebleness. Let him alone. Let him wait till the frame begins to open and the muscles to set. Meantime, keep him in the open air. His athletic sports and exercises ought to be indulged in at a later age. It is a fact that there are many men who have passed long years in a semi-state of "weediness", who have settled down in life, but whom, even now, outdoor life and exercise would convert into strong men. The tendency to physical development is as pronounced in the apparently feeble as in those who at once show their full power. Do not judge a man too soon.

5

We are in fact a slow-growing people. By law, on attaining to twenty-one years, the youth becomes a man. Physically, it is by no means so. He may be: nay, he always is, a man; but he has not nearly reached his full growth. Twenty-six or -seven years is really much nearer the truth, and many do not "set" (excepting those who live by manual labour) till thirty. Even then, growth is not concluded. The body becomes firmer, broader, thicker; there is an increase of solidness. At forty years of age numberless men are only just in their full manhood. They are then capable of harder work, or more prolonged exercise, and of enduring more fatigue, than in the flush of youth. Ours is a race which naturally tends to produce veterans. An ideal training system, therefore, should look forward to six-and-thirty, or forty, as its object. And our reliance should be on those who are tending to the prime of life. For reasons which will presently appear, this is a most encouraging fact. All through middle age it is common to see men enjoying robust vigour; at sixty and seventy, and even beyond that to the verge of four-score, some few display evidence of great physical power.

The records of athletic sports contain instances beyond number of the extraordinary strength and staying power attained by those who possessing great natural abilities improved them by cultivation. Say from the days of Captain Barclay only to the present, what a wonderful history might be compiled of strength and endurance. Whether in running, rowing, walking, lately swimming, the same qualities are displayed, i.e. immense vigour with the power to stay; that is, to go through the feat unwearied, and often to emerge almost as fresh as when it was commenced.

This is another form of that strength in repose which is so highly admired in the pose of the ancient statues. If I do not enlarge more fully on this part of my theme, it is because, in the first place, the facts are so incontrovertible; and, secondly, because although these instances are valuable they are not solitary. The English monarch who lost a great captain in warfare said he had in England "five hundred good as he". In like manner, the point upon which I would lay stress is not the individual achievement but the general excellence.

These men have exulted in strength, but the same tendency exists in the entire race. We carry the same inherent power wherever we go; thus the Australians come from the antipodes every now and then and make a gallant battle on a greensward, or the waterway with us. It is bred in the blood and it comes out.

The facts being so patent it is not necessary to trace them to their causes, were such a thing possible. But it may be observed that all the races who have resorted to these islands have been conspicuous for size or strength. The Britons were a large-limbed race; the Romans who came next had a genius for conquest; the Saxons hardiest of all; the Danes fierce and fearless; the Normans dauntless in the field; these were our ancestors. From them we have inherited tendencies which nothing can ever eradicate. Circumstances may restrain, or repress, but never extinguish them.

It is admitted that the greatest success has always followed a close observance of nature; what deduction, then, is obvious from this physical formation? Looking at such a man as a man—as an animal, if you like—apart from all moral, social, or casuistical considerations, what does his form distinctly proclaim? If you had before you a life-like statue of an Englishman, not a fanciful production or a repeated model, but an actual representation, what would you say? The statue might be regarded calmly, and without any of that sophistical blindness which will not see. What does that breadth of shoulder, that solid chest and torso, that mighty and that great hand, declare? The reply is inevitable. He was made to dig, to chop, and, if necessary, to fight.

THE SQUIRE AND THE LAND

I

"A MAN should be straight, like a gun,"* said the Squire, looking into the lock he was cleaning, and carefully running some oil which had become thick from absorbing particles of dust. "But good form is not much regarded in these days. A high score is the one great aim and object, and if you cannot make a high score there seems a feeling abroad that you may as well at once disappear. In fact, you *do* disappear. Whether it is shooting, or cricket, or lawn tennis, or boating, or swimming, or walking, you must do something that nobody else has ever done. You must kill every pigeon, or finish the mile in two seconds less time than all who have tried before. How you walk, or how you shoot, in good style or not, matters not the least. The record is everything. Nobody looks at you—the public look at the scoring board. But I like to see a man himself, as straight as a gun; what do I care about figures on the telegraph! I never could back a horse unless I had seen him, and felt him, and watched him at exercise and got to know him. There are thousands put on horses which the backers have never seen and never will see. I do not protest against it: all I say is, it is not my feeling. In the ferocious competition of our times, the competitor himself is quite forgotten. Why should everyone compete? Why enter every colt for the Derby? We seem to be all rubbed out—ourselves, I mean—and merely

* This sentence, the only one in the essay previously printed, appears in "An English Deer Park" in *Field and Hedgerow*.

143

ticketed with a number, like the convicts: a number indicating our position in the huge rush for a place. It is open to me to grumble, since I am nowhere: merely an 'O' in the world's estimation."

He polished away at the lock-plate till it shone like silver.

"As you dislike competition, some people would say you are an enemy to progress," said his visitor.

"That is the popular opinion, I know," replied the Squire. "To be a landowner is to be the bodily present-ment of ignorance and anti-civilization. I utterly deny it. I say I am an agent of rural advancement. I have done everything I could to get the school at ...* into work-ing order, short of teaching myself. I have subscribed a considerable sum towards the new railway, to meet the preliminary expenses, and parted with my land for nothing—practically nothing. Besides all my⁴ personal efforts, there's a heap of letters on the table there now waiting to be answered. Country railways would never be made without the assistance of landowners: how could the little villages and market towns pay for them? Sir Anthony N. put down a thousand, to begin with. Of course, we shall reap a benefit from it, but not nearly so much in proportion as the labouring people, whose wages will rise: they know that; they are most eager for it. My great hope is that the population will increase. I mean, our country population. There might then be a market for vegetables and garden produce, and a better demand for land to cultivate. There can scarcely be said to be a demand for land at all at the present moment."

"But, I thought," said his visitor, "that you country

* A blank in the manuscript.

gentlemen hated all innovation, and change, and would not have the railway near your parks and covers."

"Well, I cannot deny that that was the case some fifty years ago," said the Squire; "but you must, in justice, own that our ancestors had no knowledge of the rail. We can look back on it; we have had fifty years' experience, and thoroughly understand it. Is it not extremely unjust, to say the least, to visit me with opprobrium because my predecessor could not foresee steam? Who could have foreseen it?—I doubt if a Bacon could. The present generation of landowners, I assure you, think very differently. You see, I am simply a capitalist whose capital consists of land instead of cash. My class of capital has not advanced so rapidly as other kinds, and I am anxious to increase the yield from it."

"Still, you are exclusive—you stand aloof from the people; you don't assist popular movements."

"I forgive you for saying that," said the Squire, "because that also is a sort of article of belief among you City gentlemen. The truth is precisely the reverse: I assist every popular movement, from a cottage flower-show to a new railway. I have just subscribed to the new Chapel schools at Latten* (I am a Churchman, you know). I really do not think I am exclusive—I mean, personally: not so much as many wealthy employers of labour in London, who give liberal wages to their men but, beyond that, know nothing of them, or of anyone else except their own class. Now, I know almost every-one in the parish; really, I think I may say, every one, and quite three-fourths of the people round the place, and I take a great interest in them, too. Do you know, I do not think the ploughman who touches his

* i.e. Swindon.

hat to me is half so servile as many well-educated persons
I have met in town who seem able to descend to any
depth of adulation to secure an invitation to a million-
aire's table."

"But you would not speak to the ploughman."

"Not speak to a ploughman!" exclaimed the Squire,
dropping a tiny screwdriver with which he was replac-
ing the lock on the stock, in amazement, and laughing.
"I should rather think I would. I would shake hands
with any honest or decent fellow in the parish; there are
not many cottages I have not been in, at one time or
another; I, or Geraldine. But then, you City people,
who know everything, do not seem to have the least
idea of the natural condition of things in the country.
You seem to think we have stood still here these last
two generations, and are, morally and socially, still in
kneebuckles and powder!"

"No, no! not quite so bad as that; but, still, there is a
wide gulf between you and the ploughman."

"I differ," said the Squire: "the social relations are not
nearly so sharply defined in our village as in cities and
their suburbs. We have all more or less a community
of interest and a common subject to talk about: the
weather, the crops, and the state of farming. The
labourers, the farmers, the dealers—everybody has
something to say about it; I take the deepest interest in
it, of course. In cities and town life there is a diversity
of trade and business; you are not all concerned in one
business, and, therefore, you are more distant, having
no public topic of conversation. But please understand
me: I am not criticizing your manners, far from it;
what I wish is to remove some of the curious misunder-
standing which exists concerning us. You must excuse

me for saying that I think the prejudice is on your side, not ours. We have no prejudice against you, or against progress and improvement, as you wrongly assume; but you have a strong prejudice against us, as if we were survivals of the barbarous ages."

"Well," said his visitor, smiling and glancing meaningly around the gun-room at the racks, and bench, and arms. "You are looking at the old guns," said the Squire: "you consider them symptoms of barbarous tastes. There I meet you face to face to the battle—I differ from you altogether. I am for all improvements and all kinds of progress—your railways, and telegraphs, and telephones, and tramways, and education, and sanitation; your artistic propaganda, even; every scientific, and artistic, and moral, and social, step forward has my hearty good wishes. At the same time, I want a man to be a man. How can he be a man without some speck of nature in him? I don't like the idea of our becoming altogether artificial. I hope something of the forest feeling—the spirit of the forest—will survive in everyone. I am sure sport is morally good for us. Whether it is hunting, or shooting, or coursing, or racing, there is something in it which lifts one out of the vapidness of life. It braces up the body, and sets the heart beating, and lights up a sparkle in the eye. Something comes out of the woods and hills and brooks and fills you inwardly with an exaltation. You feel like a man. Fortunately, no amount of artificiality is likely to drive the love of sport out of us—out of the masses, I mean. Racing is more popular than ever; so is coursing; so is hunting; so is shooting—where one hunted years ago, ten hunt now; where one gun was sold then, twenty are sold now. People burst out every autumn; away they go to moor and loch, and sea and mountain (for climbing comes within what I call sport), to get their manhood back again.

"If ever it should happen that our forests and hills should be cultivated, and every trace of wildness smoothed out of the country, do you know, I verily believe it would become necessary to plant forests and lay down hills with turf: in short, to make national preserves—just as it is found necessary now to preserve open spaces. No: you can't rub manhood out of the English people, as the latter Romans rubbed away their beards with pumice stone.

"There is, I think, nothing so grand as the way in which the nation starts to its feet the moment there is a call to arms: let it but suppose itself insulted: let the trumpet sound, and every man is up in a second. I verily believe that in case of real danger we could raise a million men in a week."

"Horrible!" his visitor exclaimed, shutting his eyes and waving his hands: "most horrible; don't speak of anything so dreadful. I see you are as barbarian as ever."

"Not so barbarous as you and your artificiality," said the Squire, warmly, bringing down his fist with a bang on the bench and making the tools jump from their places. "Your modern ideal of women is disgraceful. I never pick up a paper without finding some evil insinuation about women. It is false, sir, false—utterly false. I say you may go into a hundred houses, one after the other, and be certain that the women are not only pure but beyond reproach. I mean to say that the tone of female society is higher and purer now than ever it was."

The Squire and the Land

2

The Squire was a good shot. He handled his double-barrel in the manner authorized by the experience of sportsmen. When a covey was flushed, or a hare started from her form, his gun came easily to the shoulder, his left hand supported it slightly in front of the trigger-guard, and, although long practice had rendered aiming in the full sense of the word unnecessary, he did not fire till the sight was on the game. There was a short but appreciable interval between the levelling of the barrel and the flash, a fatal moment of adjustment, and this calm in effort seemed to control success, for he rarely missed. The bird fell without folding her wings; the hare stopped not to sit up but to lie limp and extended.

Perhaps the most eager time in shooting is when you look through the smoke to see what has been effected. Hardly any length of practice will quite efface the sense of expectation: the gunner must look, even if he know he has killed.

The Squire's anticipation was often fulfilled; yet he did miss, and that many more times in the course of a day than sportsmen in this somewhat boastful age care to acknowledge. There seems a feverish dread lest the certainty of success should be broken by the failure of a single cartridge: a tension and anxiety as if such an incident were intolerable guilt.

The Squire's field education was completed before this fierce gamble of competition began. He did not feel that he had fallen out of the front rank even if now and then both barrels sent their contents whistling wide into the uninjured air. I think he enjoyed the stubble all the more.

This old-fashioned spirit, antecedent to the modern ideas of machine-precision, rather revolted from the patent shooting recently exhibited. Curiosity was excited, but the Squire did not much admire and was entirely devoid of emulation. Yet it quite upset all his philosophy of the gun, and perhaps that was why he did not like it. The delivery of a thousand rifle bullets pattering in succession on glass balls jerked into the air, infallibly shattering these bubbles as they rose over-threw all tradition. The bitterness was in the extreme simplicity of the trick: that no one ever thought of it. Apart, of course, from practice and natural dexterity, it merely consists in extending the left arm to nearly its full reach and holding the barrel close to the muzzle. On the appearance of the game, at once grasp the gun with the left hand, as high up the barrel as possible without inconveniently straining the muscles, and lift the left hand first, so that the muzzle may come up to the "present" a moment before the right hand brings the butt to the shoulder. All depends on the left hand, which is the centre of this method, and which must be thrust out at the mark much the same as if it grasped a pistol.

To understand the new exercise correctly, try the experiment of holding the gun steady at the "present" in this way, and, while keeping the left hand still, lower the right, letting the butt drop several inches and then raising it again. While the muzzle thus remains pointed by the left hand, the least motion of the right hand completes the position: the right, indeed, has little to do except to pull the trigger. Thumb and fingers may meet round the barrels, if preferred, for still greater stability of the left hand, as that is somewhat easier to the muscles than when the palm is hollowed but the fingers are only partly closed. Seize the barrels firmly and push the muzzle up against the mark, just as if the muzzle were going to actually touch it. Thus, the left hand aims: in the most literal sense, positively putting the muzzle on the game.

With the double-barrel shotgun no sight is required; the hand need not be bent or one eye shut, or any process of aiming gone through at all. Simply seize the barrels as near the top as convenient to the length of the arm when not unnaturally stretched, raise the barrels the fraction of a moment before the butt, look fixedly at the game, and pull the trigger: the quicker, the better. Once more let it be repeated, all is centred on the left hand: the left hand must at once, with the very first movement, take hold, high up, and must not be slid there presently; the left hand must be lifted earliest; the left hand must be thrust out at and as if it were put on the game; the left hand aims. (Educate the left arm: teach it to correspond instantaneously with the direction of the glance; teach it to be absolutely stable for the three necessary seconds; let the left hand be your top sight; let the mind act through your left wrist. With practice, such snap-shooting is possible, as has been seen in our fields.)

The trick is not in the least difficult, though so opposite to all former ideas, which attached no special value to the left hand except as a support. To attain the greatest stability consistent with ease, the usual position of the left hand is just in front of, or, with some, partly over, the trigger-guard, much about the centre of gravity of the gun. This minimizes the weight: the barrels and the stock are balanced. The new position abolishes the balance altogether—at first it seems peculiar, but soon becomes natural: and thus the most cherished traditions of shooting are put aside.

With a rifle, some little modification of these instructions is necessary. There being but one pellet, it must be delivered with accuracy, and the top sight is of the utmost importance. That a full view of it may be obtained, the thumb and fingers of the left hand must not meet, as is permissible when shooting with the double-barrel. It should be hollowed, the barrel resting on it exactly as in the old position, but must be as near the muzzle as compatible with common sense: the nearer, the better. In every other respect, the new method, with the rifle, is precisely the same as in the gun. The left hand puts the top sight at once on the mark, with such precision and ease that, with practice, a running hare or rabbit could certainly be hit. The quicker the trigger is pressed, the better: here, again, the new method directly traverses tradition. A slow, deliberative rifleman was always considered, and often with good reason, as the most successful; but, with the new position, fire cannot be delivered too quickly—the very instant the top sight is on the mark—thus converting the rifleman into a snapshooter. Instead of searching about for the mark, like an astronomer for some faint star with his telescope, as was usually the case under the old style, in the new, the muzzle, the top sight, is put immediately on it, held there rigid, and the bullet has done its work before an old style rifleman could have got his weapon comfortably settled at his shoulder.

The thing is capable of mathematical demonstration.

Anyone, however, may convince himself of the fact by a simple experiment with a walking-stick. Take the crook or knob in the right hand and place that hand upon the table. This represents the butt of the gun pressed to the shoulder, which is the fixed point. Put the thumb and finger of the left hand on the stick, about a third of its length, reckoning from the right. Then you have the gun held in the ordinary position. Now, while retaining the right hand still (as the shoulder would be), move the left hand laterally either way an inch or so. An inch of movement at the left hand causes thrice the deflection at the fore end of the stick. A mere sixteenth of an inch trebles itself there—the angle widens. This initial error in the aim goes on increasing, every yard, till at the mark forty yards away the largest spread of shot fails of effect. On a smaller scale, the same experiment may be carried out with a cedar pencil, and always with the same result: the closer the left hand is placed to the right, the more a slight initial movement increases the error (or widens the angle) at the top, or muzzle.

On the reverse, the opposite effect is produced. While still holding the crook or knob of the stick steady with the right hand, extend the left arm and place the thumb and finger on the stick as near the top as you conveniently can. Then you have the new position. It now requires a large lateral motion of the left hand to produce an error or divergence equal in extent to that which previously resulted from the least movement. The muzzle, or top of the stick, only varies from the straight line to the amount of the actual movement of the left hand; in the former case, a slight error of the hand multiplied itself at the muzzle.

As the arm is not a mechanical rest of iron which can be fixed irrespective of circumstances, but is endowed with feeling, with a beating pulse, muscles that relax or contract in response to the variation of the will, and is therefore uncertain in its action, anything that reduces these vibrations to a minimum must improve the shooting. The object is to get the eye, the top sight of the rifle or the muzzle of the gun, and the game, all three distinctly in a line with each other. When holding the gun, as the walking-stick was first held, say, at a third of its length, the muzzle has to go searching about for the mark. If practice brings up the gun true in general direction, still it has to be adjusted; and, when adjusted, the faintest error of the arm is doubled at the muzzle.

So that the new position is not only correct mathematically, it is best suited to the practical difficulties of shooting. You do not seem to depend on the gun, but simply on the left hand. You stretch out your left hand and, as it were, put it on the mark, and immediately fire.

All this applies, of course, to sporting only: that is, to shooting at short ranges. At the long distance target it would not answer. It applies also only to quick shooting. It is not possible to shoot slowly in the new position, not meaning the number of discharges but the time occupied in aiming. If anyone wishes to make a steady, slow aim, the old position is best. Indeed, it is scarcely possible to aim long—to dwell on the aim—in the new way: the arm extended very nearly to its full length soon begins to quiver a little; and when once the vibration begins it cannot be quite stopped unless it is lowered for a moment. When first raised, the muzzle is at once put on the mark; the arm retains it there, then fire—whether shotgun or rifle.

As most sporting, even with the improved rifles, takes place at short range, the value of the new method appears very high. One caution it is as well to add: and that is, not to try this plan except with a perfectly trustworthy gun. Since breech-loading has become universal, guns burst less frequently, as it is not possible to double charge, and the barrels can be looked through lest any dirt should choke them. But, even now, guns do burst occasionally.

I have no possible grounds upon which to go, but I have long had a faint suspicion that, since breech-loading was adapted to every gun, many guns have been turned out only just thick enough in the metal to bear the expected strain, and without any provision, as it were, against the chance of extra pressure. As the left hand is much exposed in the new position, let no one use it unless quite certain of his gun.

When a lad, I often used to shoot sparrows at a trap, and became very expert at it; and I remember that my success was due to the manner in which I held the gun, grasping it before giving the signal with the left hand where that hand would have to sustain it when at the shoulder. The difference was that not a second was lost in the adjustment of the left hand or support, and it had not to be slid into position. There was nothing to do but to keep the eyes fixed on the ground about six inches in front of the trap, give the signal, fling up the gun, and pull the trigger. This was, in a measure, an approach to the new position. But then all the sparrows started from the same spot. The new position puts the muzzle of the double-barrel at

once on the flying game, just as if the top touched the
partridge.

3

"There are not ten acres on this estate," wrote the
Squire, "that could be better farmed than at present.
The woods perhaps might, theoretically, be ploughed
and planted, but in fact they occupy the worst part of
the property, and, if cut down, any practical farmer
will tell you, would only make thin hillside grazing
ground. The strip of marshy pasture in the bottom
below cannot be drained unless the little lake or pond
were emptied, to do which the county, or the govern-
ment, must construct a canal several miles long.

"As commercial principles are to be applied to land-
owning, on a balance of profit and loss, the woods, as
they stand, pay well. In proportion to the labour
employed, the return is high. There are, however, some
outlying copses which could be spared, and which
stand on good land: in all, I think they equal about
twenty acres. The tenants would object, as they would
have to pay much higher for poles, flukes, hurdles, and
all the endless wood used on farms, if every ash and
hazel stole were grubbed.

"I have no hesitation in asserting that if the manage-
ment of the estate were vested in a council of the
tenants they would carefully provide for the retention
of a large extent of wood.

"The American who was over here last spring told
me that the farmers in his country always set aside so
much of their farms for the growth of timber. It is
found to be absolutely necessary.

"I keep up a good head of pheasants, but I do not

think I am extravagant in proportion to the acreage of wood. Some people object to pheasants on sentimental grounds: well, they can certainly point the finger at me in this respect. But the tenants make no grievance of it —I have had no complaint whatever since I gave up the rabbits about ten years ago. They have the hares, too, after September; that is, after my party has been round. We are on the best of terms, but still there is an indefinite something in the air which pushes on the attack upon the land, and most people who have property recognize the cloud in the sky which, like the dust raised by an army, presages the assault.

"For my part, if anyone can suggest to me a plan by which more can be got out of the land, the tenants rendered prosperous, the labourers better off, and in a general sense more advantageous to the country, I will welcome him with open arms. The lawyers may put difficulties in his way: not I. But there are two things to which I will never consent: I will not consent to my own abolition, and I will not part with a single yard of ground. That premised, I will cordially assist any attempt to increase the production.

"The advocates of Land Reform all seem to start from the supposition that the landowners are a party of obstruction: that they will oppose every project of improvement. I deny this most emphatically. If they can propose any legislation short of abolishing me, or actually taking my land from me, I shall make no opposition. A prospect of getting more out of the land would, on the contrary, fill me with delight. But I want an answer to this question: what can you do with the land more than has already been done?

"I do not believe there is a single thing that has been

recommended that has not been tried on my property. The turnips come first: it is a long time ago now; still, they may be said to represent, in agriculture, what steam represents in commerce, i.e., forward motion. Certainly we have grown turnips enough, and other roots in vast quantities, and continue to do so, but we cannot do any more with them than we have done. We shall not cease to produce roots, but the limit of what can be effected with roots has been reached.

"Improvement of animal shape was the next great step: we were instructed to produce both sheep and cattle perfect[17] in form. That, too, has been done. We ourselves have done it here—Butler, up on the Downs, has taken a whole list of prizes for sheep; that American I alluded to came over on purpose to purchase some of the breed. And Thorn, whom you will remember (he's not the largest tenant but he's a monied man) has been equally successful with his shorthorns. His holding is on our arable plain. Shorthorns—what a volume of departed hope might not be written about them! They have been the Brighton "A" Stock of Agriculture—the subject of wildest speculation, now up, now down, fluctuating not on intrinsic value but on mere opinion.

"So we have done all that can be done with sheep and cattle. We shall still keep sheep and cattle, but the limit of what can be effected with improved breeds has been reached.

"Suppose the State owned this property and brought the vast revenue collected in England to bear upon it: suppose a million per annum were spent here in improving our sheep and cattle, we should get no further. Millions have already been expended by private individuals, and, what is of more value than mere money,

time, skill, and, in its way, genius. The practical limit has been reached.

"Steam-ploughing ranks next. We have used the steam-plough. My father, as you know, was especially interested in the steam-plough. He spent time and money on it, and gave every facility to tenants who wished to try it. Thorn has a pair of engines and tackle, and in fine weather I constantly hear them at work. My father fancied the steam-plough particularly suited to our local arable plain; and there's no doubt it did some good. But then, you see, we have got the steam-plough, and we can't go any further. If the State itself were the owner of Thorn's farm, it could not employ more than one set of tackle on it. The limit of what can be done with the steam-plough has been reached.

"It is the same with guano. We have been rather more lavish with manure than is customary, as we found it answer as well as, or better than, anything. All the tenants used it, till their losses compelled them to reduce expenditure; and even now they are using as much as ever again in hope of recouping themselves. Still, we cannot go any further. Beyond a certain quantity it is no use putting any more.

"As for draining, all the draining that could be done has been done; in some places I am told we have over-done the draining, and we are rather discouraged with it. That is because so much of the land here drains itself sufficiently—a thing we did not appreciate until we had tried our hands at improving Nature, and failed. I say 'we' advisedly, for my father, five-and-thirty years, perhaps forty years, ago began to work with his tenants in these things. They have had to pay rent, of course; but they have practically governed the estate as much as if they had formed a council board. All their ideas have been carried out, so far as was practicable, for you know that matters are very different, when you come to deal with substantial things like land, than the theory looks on paper. I have gone on with the same system. There's nothing peculiar in it: ours is not a solitary instance; in fact, every owner I know, with the exception of two or three who are in pecuniary difficulties, is now doing the same,   not from sentimental reasons but because they believe it the most profitable policy.

"Well! now I want to know what can you do with the land more than has already been done?

"Simultaneously with these purely farming steps in advance, general improvements have taken place all over the property. My father established a sort of sinking-fund for these purposes—it was (and is) the rent from two small dairy farms he chanced to inherit unexpectedly. Every year the rent from these has been steadily applied to the building of new cattle-sheds, enlargement of farm-houses, making new roads, putting up fresh cottages, and you would be surprised at what has been effected in this way in the process of time.

"Capital sums have also been expended for the same ends at intervals, and I really do not think any reasonable request has been refused: my father refused to put in some bow windows to a farmstead; and I myself refused to build a tenant a new house, in fact a villa, his idea being that his bailiff could live in the old one.

"I own that many of the cottages in . . .* are defective: I don't think there is any serious sanitary fault, for, fortunately, there is plenty of pure spring water—which

* A blank in the manuscript.

is so great an advantage to a village. I cannot rebuild the whole place: the State itself could not do it, without heavily taxing somebody; and, even then, could not let expensive buildings at the extremely low rental within the agricultural labourers' means.

"There are plenty of allotments, and always have been ever since I can remember. Wages are not high—the tenants think them too high—but I am writing from the broadest point of view, and I must say that wages are not high. I do not think I can alter that. Even the State itself could not fix the rate of wages.

"I am not so bigoted but that I can see a great deal of creaking in the machinery of our agricultural life—hard work and not too bountiful food, and trouble, and so on. But what am I to do? Am I a demi-god? What could the State itself do? For everything human is more or less crank.

"Lastly, everybody told us that we ought to remit the rent: but I will leave that to my next letter."

4

"Everybody insisted, as I said before," the Squire continued, "that we ought to remit the rent. We *did* remit the rent. If the State had been landlord, instead of me, what more could it have done? I remitted my rent; but one thing is quite certain, the State did *not* remit its rent. A very cruel and exacting taskmaster, *sans compassion*, is the State. In the year of deepest depression, we were called upon for rates and taxes just the same as in the most profitable season. This should not be forgotten by those who are so anxious to have the State as their landlord.

The Squire and the Land

"I think you will now admit that we have tried everything; that we have done everything practicable with the land that could be done; and that the limit has been reached. Two remedies alone remain, over one of which we have no power, and to the other (if it is a remedy) I will never consent. One is the removal of the taxation which presses so heavily on the land: the other is communism. The first would undoubtedly prove a great relief, though I do not think it would effect everything (see what I shall say presently about the Market); and I want to know how long other portions of the community would consent to one class alone being freed from taxation! There would soon be an outcry. If the remission of taxation was only partial, then I say deliberately that it would not be effectual. As to communism, I will be guillotined before I will consent to it.

"How completely outside our feelings are those who talk so glibly of compensation! They say: 'You would be well paid for the land taken from you to be sub-divided among the people at large.' Now, how utterly void of understanding us must be those who suggest that money would repay us! How *can* they compensate us? We have held part of this estate since the time of Henry . . .* and the rest since Edward VI. Just consider a moment what root we have taken in all these years! If you plant shrubs in a nursery garden, you plant them to sell, and money will compensate you for their removal. But we did not plant our trees to sell. We like to see them increase and flourish, and, by and by, to watch their slow decay. I declare that a hollow old oak is a noble sight.

* A blank in the manuscript.

"Here I take my stand! By main force I may be abolished—not otherwise. Only I wish it to be well understood that I, and others in my position, are not a party of obstruction, as it pleases certain people to suppose us. Any legislation, any suggestion you or anybody

else can put forward to improve the condition of the tenants, the labourers, the village, the land itself, I shall welcome with open arms.

"But I do not think anything practical remains to be proposed. As for the abolition of primogeniture, the easier   transfer of land, the repeal of the landlord's right as first creditor, these are mere side-issues and blind alleys, and would not, if granted, cause one single extra ear of wheat to be grown, nor give us one single extra shilling   per quarter. The lawyers seem determined to fight for these matters, inch by inch: and well they may, since they obtain so rich a harvest as the custodians of our titles. I cannot say that I care much: perhaps I do not understand these subtleties. I do, however, doubt whether the repeal of my right as first creditor in case of a tenant's bankruptcy would be much to the farmer's advantage. It would only enable him to borrow a little more, and already the tenant farmers are deep enough in debt. If the only way to get more capital put into the soil is to enlarge facilities for borrowing, we had better be without it.

"So I do not think anything practical remains to be proposed. The American who came over to buy some sheep of Butler—he was quite a gentleman, and we had many conversations—well, I asked him if he could suggest anything. He went all over the place, and he considered, and said there was but one thing—would I take offence? I said: 'Certainly not.' 'Well then, Squire,' said he: 'the only thing I can see is to get rid of *you*!' I asked him, in reply, whether it was not true that farmers in the United States were in the hands of the money-lender and were paying him such interest that it amounted to a rent. He owned it was true, but hit me in return: for, he added, 'the tenant here pays the money-lender, as in the United States, but also pays the landlord.' But I went on to ask who, if I were abolished, was to occupy my place. He said: 'Of course, the State—that vague, impersonal corporation.' And then I asked: 'If a man emigrates to America, does he find a substantial stone or brick built homestead, ranges of solidly constructed, slated cattle-sheds, well cultivated fields, trimmed hedges, good private roads: in short, a ready-made farm waiting for him as a free present from the State on his arrival?' My friend smiled

sarcastically, and said: 'That kind of thing costs dollars.'
Then I pointed out that the State here would not supply
such farms for nothing: the tenants must borrow the
capital to buy them, and the interest on that capital
would equal the rent paid to me; they must, too,
borrow the capital to put stock on and to work it, and
the interest on that would represent the money-lender.
I fancy they would find the State and the money-lender
harder landlords than me. Money-lenders are not
renowned for sympathy, or for consideration towards
their debtors. They are not famous for remitting *their*
rents, that is, their interest: still less when they deem
their capital in danger—for the right of first creditor is
to be repealed. Certainly the State does not remit its
rent: most certainly the State insists on its right as first
creditor.

"My American friend was candid enough to own
that it was rather more of a tangle than it looked: the
brambles grew so thick, said he, in the old country—
you could not move without catching your foot in one.
Still, he seemed to have a lingering desire to see me got
rid of: he evidently had a feeling that I was in the way.
I do not deny it. I know I am in the way. So, too, the
farmer is in the way of the labourer; and the labourer,
with his cottage and garden, is in the way of the tramp
along the road, who has none, and would much like to
take the loaf from the shelf within—only the labourer
has locked the door. Just so! I am in the way; and I
will not consent to my own abolition. I will not consent to communism—neither, I am certain, would my
American friend, who had so high an opinion of dollars
but not the slightest desire to share them with other
people.

The Squire and the Land

"But, though I will not consent to communism, it is a great mistake to suppose that I object to the sub-letting of the land, to the multiplication of homesteads, to the increase of the rural population. Precisely the reverse! If I could get five hundred tenants on the estate instead of fifty, my income would be trebled. I should be only too glad to split every farm up into allotments and let every single acre to a separate tenant at allotment rentals. Why, I should indeed be rich! Only let a thousand people apply to me for an acre each, and they shall have it. By Jove, I should think so! The idea is too ravishingly pleasant to dream of. Look, too, at the influence it would give me—like a colliery, or iron-works, or cotton-mills. I assure you, I will give every facility. I would go to Parliament for a Private Act, if necessary. Send me the thousand tenants quick!—But no. No such thing. The world is old, and the general sense of the public not to be so deceived. Even the masses who have had no experience of farming instinctively know better: else the mechanics from Leeds and Birmingham would come crowding down here and squat on my land, like the gold-diggers. I wish to heaven they would! A very small royalty would satisfy me. But, though they have had these things preached at them for so many years, they instinctively know better. Every man's sense tells him that my estate has nothing to offer him. Beechmast and acorns are not gold dust. If only someone could discover a plant which would yield a monetary return when cultivated in plots like large gardens, then the difficulty would be solved. The thousand tenants would soon be a fact, and the land question would settle itself. But grapes will not flourish: nor olive trees, nor figs; tobacco, they say,

might be grown, to some extent, but the excise is heavy
—nor could we hope to compete with Virginia. As for
fruit and vegetables—fruit is the most uncertain of
crops; for vegetables, there is not sufficient demand.
Just in the neighbourhood of cities, it may answer; but
not over the country at large. Therefore, I do not see
how small tenants or acre-farmers are ever to succeed.
But it is not true that I oppose their introduction.

"Our only reason in favour of large farms was, and
is, that wheat and meat can best be produced on a large
scale. In fact, you cannot profitably produce them on a
small one. In America I read of wheat-fields so immense
that it occupies a   team an entire day to cross them—an
entire day to plough a single furrow! How is an acre-
farmer to compete with that? Large farmers with considerable capital cannot do it; and the fact is recognized
by reformers, who advise us to grow strawberries,
beetroot for sugar, to establish distilleries for mangold
spirit, and many other things of like character, which
possibly might prove successful if we could be as sure
of sunshine as they are abroad. Instead of which, the
more meteorological observations are made, the more
uncertain our climate is found to be.

"Nevertheless,   it is not the weather nor the seasons
that has depressed us: such seasons have happened
before, and even worse, and we have risen again. But,
in those days, there was practically no America. By
slow degrees, the imports of corn and other foods have
brought us on our knees. We cannot compete against it
under any imaginable system. The wheat average, as
published at this moment, is about 42s. But it is well
known that the average, so-called, is fixed too high:
and much corn has been sold at 36s., that is, 18s. a sack.

The Squire and the Land

In short, to sum up in a word, it is the Market that is the cause of our difficulties.

"The Market is down, and will remain down, and we are down with it. Sub-divide, split up the land as you will—drive me out by main force—but you cannot live against that Market. The greatest fallacy I have seen is the argument some have put forth that, by and by, the Americans will not find it possible to produce wheat to sell to us at a profit, on account of the increased cost of production and their own extraordinary increase of population. The reverse is the fact. The more their population increases, the more wheat and meat they send us; and at a cheaper price, because the means of communication are extended. The fact is, they must grow wheat, whether it pays or not; it is the only thing they can grow for which they can get ready cash.

"From what the American gentleman told me, I understand that for years past this has been the case. In a different way, they are in the same predicament that we are: we do not know what to produce but wheat and meat; nor do they, only they have the whip hand of us. On their immense quantities, too, a very slight percentage pays.

"I think that, as the means of communication are increased, wheat and meat will come to us cheaper and cheaper, not only from America but from all parts of the world. All other matters, in comparison, are trifles —it is the Market that rules us.

"In conclusion, I have only to repeat that, if I am driven out by main force, the State will be found a harsher landlord than the Squire. If the land is divided into fractions, the produce from it will immediately be diminished by at least a third. The great wheat countries will then not only have the whip hand of us: they will put the bit in our mouths. For it is the production of English wheat and meat—produced at a terrible cost of capital, time, skill, care, and in face of every discouragement,   that has hitherto compelled the foreigner to sell cheap to undersell us. He does not benevolently sell cheap for the good of Leeds and Birmingham. If he could get rid of us, if the English farmer were suppressed altogether, loud would be his rejoicings, as he could then sell dear.

"I ask: What more can be done with the land than has already been done? Give me a suggestion, and I will welcome it   cordially. I am the willing agent of improvement, ready with capital and sympathy: I am not a party of obstruction; nor am I inexorable, like the State. This is my case."

THE LIFE OF THE SOUL

I

THE dawn to me is when I open my eyes, and my first thought is of my prayer, repeated by that thought, the same prayed on the hills and everywhere else so long.

The light is the first thing I see, and by the light I say: Give me the reality of the feeling, which comes into existence with life. I am awakened and I live, give me that fullness of existence which I have so long desired and the idea of which is given by the light and by every loveliness of the earth.

But the sun has been up for many hours, and the summer day is already far advanced. I feel that I have lost these hours, this light and beauty which has been pouring over the wheat and the meadows, over the woods and sea, all this time while I not only did nothing but was unconscious of it—while I may be strong enough to grasp the whole beauty of the day from dawn till evening cannot I take it all? Must I always feel that it has been going by me like a stream?

The wheat-ear as it turns yellow has taken the sunlight and the beauty into itself. So I would take the beauty into myself.

But I have the same desire when there is nothing about me—nothing but walls—when I cannot see the outside earth or the sunlight—the same desire in my mind; it is like a thirst of the mind, like a drawing-in the breath for this beauty in itself. It does not exist as a separate thing, I know, but I desire that which answers to it—which I read from it—in my mind. The letters or the words of a book are nothing—but the thought they give is real. The sunlight and the wheat-ear are the letters and the word: the thought that comes is real; and I feel it when they are not visible.

My mind prays, turning in on itself, apart from all things. The pressure of every day, of doing things, puts it aside, but if I stay still as it were for a moment and think of myself, the same wish returns unending, though the surroundings of the moment be commonplace and dusty enough. The thought runs winding through my days.

It is in me and within the sunbeam, or the wheat-ear, or the grass. In the secret, separate entity of the soul, wishing, impelled to it, it almost represents or is my soul. The moment I think of myself it comes again, however long pushed aside by work or sense matters. It will therefore be always there, unceasingly praying.

Why have I not gone forth for this soul life, searching for it more in the forest and by the sea?

That I may see through the sunlight and the earth, the enclosure with which the mind is surrounded, the wall, into the depth of the soul behind. These are like a solid arch over and the eyes are apt to stay at them; let me see beyond, deeper through. It is not the air that blows over the dry, rustling barley; not the warm sunshine; not the earth with the flowers; not the water, nor the light; it is the thing beyond, which I would see and feel.

That I cannot pray high enough—cannot put my desire into an idea high enough—cannot find an idea high enough to say this is it, this is what I really mean —I cannot imagine it.

The Life of the Soul

I wish to do more than has ever been done since the beginning—since the first man walked into the sun—since the first naked foot pressed on the dust—to do higher, not mechanical things only, but in myself—as flesh and blood.

The first discovery was the existence of the soul, the second, its immortality, the third, the Deity. Give me to make a fourth discovery beyond these. There must be something else to know. There is something through the earth and sun, on the other side. Nothing satisfies me unless I can discover this—I always return to this and must do it.

These thoughts, they are almost inexpressible, have haunted my mind, from the early days at Coate, until now.

2

If the idle day will come, let hope and faith in it be always like the air.

That such a breath may come to the mind is the desire, the hope, and the prayer. Part of the brain still sleeps, that part of it used in the re-learning of ancient thoughts is scarcely half stored. The rest sleeps.

There is not one of us but has a mind-power of which he hardly dreams. Touching a flower, we seem as if we were absorbing something of this dormant mind-power. It flows from the flower, like its odour. The perfume of the flower cannot be written. The violet cannot be expressed in words, though it is material. There is no language, yet, to express the feeling which flows from the flower. From the touch of the green sward a feeling flows as if the great earth sent a mystic perfume—an immaterial influence—through the frame.

More of this influence: more and more; it cannot be translated, yet, but it can be felt. Some day it will be translated; it is like hovering on the verge of a great truth.

We can only get at the immaterial through the material. How many books must be written to explain it; and, even then, would it be explained!

So that the thought that there is more yet for the mind can be put in a sentence, but requires pages to explain. It is not that the mind is limited and cannot understand: it is that the facts have not yet been put before it. Like a lens, the mind can only examine that which is passed before it. Those things which are dimly shadowed forth by the flower, the leaf, the very touch of earth—which are felt, rather than perceived—have not yet been put before it. They have not been defined, and brought into shape, so as to admit of being weighed and arranged.

Remaining content on a mental level is fatal to all progress of thought. Saying to ourselves, "There is nothing more: this is our limit," is the loss and ruin of the mind.

Lift up. Lift up! look higher! The little is so heavy that it is often an effort to escape it. Alas for the twisted skein of life.

Pity indeed it is that the larger part of the mind should be idle and worthy the object to find more for it.

Forwards, because the time that I possess in advance must shorten day by day.

The truth is, we do not understand our own earth yet: our own life. It is visible and tangible, like the leaf emerging from the bud, many books have been written on it, still it is unsolved.

The Life of the Soul

If these are but vague aspirations, they insensibly direct the mind; unseen but strong.

Many of us have partially recognized the existence of a current of unconscious thought, which gradually works its way and decides our course, even against our own waking decisions. We get a glimpse of such a current now and then, and lose sight of it again.

So long ago is it since the first promptings of these thoughts arose in my mind that it is difficult to trace the beginnings of them. They spread abroad downwards like the roots of a tree, and the deeper they are sought out the more finely divided they appear and difficult to detach from the earth. To the very base of life they go.

The blue hill-line arouses another such perception; it is like looking through a window into a part of ourselves we do not always see.

We can see ourselves partly by looking back on our past life.

The feeling caused by the view of flower and distant hill-line—the very touch of the green sward—is it not a recognition of our own life? It is seeing—feeling the existence of the soul—in the midst of the stream of light—in the way of the rush of wind.

In daily routine and work we really forget ourselves. Here the light and air recalls us. Give us more of our inner selves: not the coarse, rude, outer covering, and its wishes, but of the inner secret existence. That inner secret existence desires nothing but beauty. But the word "beauty" is weak to carry the feeling meant.

Those who have ever experienced the depth of this feeling must perforce pray with every glimpse of sunlight and of the unknown beyond.

More books from Ex Libris Press:

THE WALKER'S COMPANION

A Collection for all who
enjoy the countryside on foot

The works of some 23 writers, beginning with Wordsworth a
ending with Henry Williamson are quoted here and all illustrate so
aspect of the walker's art. The urge to get away from it all and get cl
to nature opens us to the varied pleasures of walking: the pursuit
health, relaxation and renewal. All these are celebrated in prose a
poetry. So too are the delights of the country footpath and mounta
track, whether they be the fruits of a day's ramble or of an extend
walking tour.

This remarkable collection of prose and verse . . . a charming ramble of a b
Wiltshire Gazette and Her

Illustrated with pen and ink sketches by Edward Dowden
A5 Paperback   112 pages   Price £2.

Down the BRISTOL AVON

Including 14 Country Walks

The Bristol Avon springs to life in the foothills of the Gloucestersh
Cotswolds. For much of its 75 miles it flows through the quiet a
peaceful countryside of North and West Wiltshire by many of
pleasant and interesting towns and villages. Included among these
the hilltop town of Malmesbury, the outstanding National Tr
village of Lacock and Bradford-on-Avon, 'the most beautiful li
town in all Wiltshire'. The Avon rolls on through the incompara
Georgian city of Bath and the once great port of Bristol. Some of
more fascinating places and personalities associated with the Av
valley are recounted. In addition, some fourteen circular walks
described by which the reader may explore, at first hand,
countryside of the Bristol Avon.

It is well-researched and well-informed both as walker's guide and histor
survey   Exploring Local Hist

Illustrated throughout with photographs, engravings and sketch ma
Uniform with *Where Wiltshire meets Somerset*   136 pages   Price £3.

Available from bookshops or post free from the publishers:
Ex Libris Press, 1 The Shambles, Bradford-on-Avon, Wiltshire